Finding CALM
in the CHAOS

KATHLEEN LONG BOSTROM

Finding CALM
in the CHAOS

Christian Devotions
for Busy Women

WJK WESTMINSTER
JOHN KNOX PRESS
LOUISVILLE · KENTUCKY

Scripture quotations from the New Revised Standard Version of the Bible are copyright © 1989 by the Division of Christian Education of the National Council of the Churches of Christ in the U.S.A. and are used by permission.

See acknowledgments, pp. 354-356, for additional permission information.

Book design by Drew Stevens
Cover design by designpointinc.com

First edition
Published by Westminster John Knox Press
Louisville, Kentucky

This book is printed on acid-free paper that meets the American National Standards Institute Z39.48 standard. ♾

PRINTED IN THE UNITED STATES OF AMERICA

05 06 07 08 09 10 11 12 13 14 — 10 9 8 7 6 5 4 3 2 1

Library of Congress Cataloging-in-Publication Data

Bostrom, Kathleen Long.
 Finding calm in the chaos : Christian devotions for busy women / Kathleen Long Bostrom.— 1st ed.
  p. cm.
Includes bibliographical references.
 ISBN 0-664-22916-6 (alk. paper)
 1. Christian women—Prayer-books and devotions—English. 2. Devotional calendars. I. Title.

 BV4844.B67 2005
 242'.643—dc22

2005042310

O, it is lovely to feel a book, a good book, firm in the hand, for its fatness holds rich promise, and you are hot inside to think of good hours to come.

—Richard Llewellyn, 464

O that my words were written down!
O that they were inscribed in a book!
O that with an iron pen and with lead
   they were engraved on a rock forever!
For I know that my Redeemer lives,
   and that at the last he will stand upon the earth.

—Job 19: 23–25

CONTENTS

INTRODUCTION

The front door slams as the last of my three children heads out the door to school. Today is one of my "work-at-home days." As a part-time pastor and a part-time writer (both of which are often full-time jobs) I use my days off from the church to work on my writing. I look forward to a quiet day alone, empty pages waiting to be covered with words. I fill the teakettle with water and click on the flame, already savoring a steaming cup of tea and a few moments of quiet before I begin to write.

I sit down at the dining room table and scan the headlines in the day's paper. About halfway down the first column, the dog starts to whine. I get up, take him downstairs to feed him, and, while in the basement, realize that there are a couple of loads of wash that need to be done. I gather up a load and toss it in the washer, then start back up the stairs. The dog whines again, and I realize that in my zeal to get the laundry started, I forgot to put the food in his bowl. Back down the stairs I go.

That done, I head up the stairs. The phone rings. Am I interested in having a new roof put on the house? No, I answer, not really, but thanks for calling. I hang up the phone and see the balls of dust that skitter across the floor as I move towards the kitchen. I get the vacuum out of the closet and suck up the little critters before they decide to join forces with all the other dust balls in the house and take over completely.

While I'm at it, I figure I might as well vacuum the rest of the upstairs. I decide to start with the kitchen. Bent over my task with utmost deliberation, it isn't until I stand up to catch my breath that I see the teakettle, which by now has sent clouds of steam throughout the room, fogging the windows. I turn off the stove, grab the teakettle with a hot pad and lift it to pour my tea, but the kettle is nearly empty, and I have to refill it and start all over again.

I quickly finish the vacuuming, stuff the vacuum back in the closet, pour my tea, and sit down to read the paper, but I've forgotten where I left off, so I decide it's too late to bother with the paper and I might as well go check my e-mail. But as soon as I sit down at the computer, the washing machine buzzer sounds, the doorbell rings, a spider sails out on an invisible thread from the corner behind the desk, and the dog is at my heels, whining to go outside. That reminds me — I need to go for a walk, too. I've been promising myself every day I'd get outside and stretch my legs. Maybe tomorrow. The day is half gone already, and I haven't written a single word.

It seems that no matter what time I get up in the morning (and I'm not a morning person to begin with), the day gets away from me before I have a chance to finish even a quarter of the tasks that demand my attention. This is the equation of my life: One husband plus two jobs plus three children plus half a dozen projects all going on at once equals a very busy life. No wonder I'm tired. Who isn't? I'm no different from most of the women I know, even though the variables in the equation may vary amongst us.

Where, in the midst of the chaos of our lives is there time for quiet reflection, prayer, Bible study, simple time with God? Too busy in the morning, too tired at night, we neglect our spiritual lives in the rush to accomplish the "necessities." Even using a daily devotional guide can add to our stress when it becomes "one more thing to do," and we are left with feelings of guilt when our good intentions about spending time nurturing our spirits get swept up and shoved in the closet along with the vacuum cleaner.

But wait—here's some good news! The devotional book you hold in your hand is written to be a stress-free way of assuring that you feed your soul along with your family. This book is intended to help you create calm in the chaos, not add to it. In the account of creation found in Genesis, chapter 1, we read that

> in the beginning when God created the heavens and the earth, the earth was a formless void and darkness covered the face of the deep, while a wind from God swept over the face of the waters. Then God said, "Let there be light"; and there was light. And God saw that the light was good.
>
> Gen. 1:1–4

Goodness can come out of chaos. New life can come out of chaos. Calm can be created out of chaos. We may not be able to snap our fingers like God and get everything in perfect order. We can, however, learn to create calm in the midst of our busy lives through the same Spirit of God that hovered over the chaos at the beginning of creation, as we allow the time and space for the Spirit to put shape and form to the disorder of our own spiritual selves.

The guidelines that follow give you a breakdown of how the book is organized and how to use the Bible readings and devotions. Don't feel bound to any rules—if you come up with other ways this book can help you find that space for God to work in your life, that's great! I think God would like that, too.

I wish you joy as you join with the Spirit of God in creating calm in the chaos. May God bless you all along the way.

HOW TO USE THIS BOOK

Finding Calm in the Chaos is organized by the months of the year. You can begin using the book during any month. Each month provides the following:

Weekly Bible Readings

Unlike devotional books that offer a separate Bible passage for each day, this devotional provides one Bible reading per week. For seven days, you read the same Bible passage, reflecting on its meaning through the daily devotions, prayers, poems, and quotations.* Each month includes a reading from the Old Testament, the Psalms, the Gospels, and the New Testament (other than the Gospels).

By reading the same passage repeatedly, you allow space for the Spirit to work. Live with the passage each day. Sink into the reading as you would a warm bath. Relax. Enjoy. Soak yourself in God's word.

Week by Week

Centering on the theme of the month and the Scripture passage for the week, each week includes:

> Day 1: Scripture passage/Spirit Boosters for the week
> Day 2: Devotion

*Every attempt was made in the writing of this book to be sensitive to the use of inclusive language. There are instances, however, when a quote, poem, or prayer written by another author includes various masculine words or images. For the most part, these words and images were left unchanged in order to respect the work of the original author.

Day 3: Poem
Day 4: Prayer
Day 5: Devotion
Day 6: Quotation
Day 7: Sabbath Celebration

Spirit Boosters

One day, Jesus was asked which was the greatest of the commandments. He replied,

> You shall love the Lord your God with all your heart, and with all your soul, and with all your mind, and with all your strength. The second is this: You shall love your neighbor as yourself. There is no other commandment greater than these.
>
> Mark 12:30–31

Jesus' commandment is twofold: to love God and to love our neighbors as ourselves—which means we have to be kind to our own selves as well as to others. To help you as you seek to fulfill this commandment, *Finding Calm in the Chaos* provides what I call "Spirit Boosters"—simple ways you can nurture your own faith even as you seek ways to offer a kindness to someone else.

The Spirit Boosters are divided into two areas: "Reaching In" and "Reaching Out." The Reaching In section offers suggestions for being kind to yourself. The section on Reaching Out offers possibilities for doing just that—reaching out to others. These Spirit Boosters are offered to encourage you to incorporate Reaching In and Reaching Out into your daily life. You may have plenty of other ideas. That's great! Add them to the list. There is an abundance of opportunities waiting to be discovered.

Prayer

You are encouraged to pray each day, using the prayers included in each week (Day Four and Day Seven—Sabbath Celebration). Your prayer can be as long or as short as it needs to be. Don't worry about having the right words. God doesn't care if your prayers are simple or detailed. There are times when what your spirit needs most is silent prayer: sitting quietly, not worrying about forming prayers with words, but allowing yourself to be in God's presence.

Sabbath Celebration

After the completion of creation, God took a day to rest. There was a time when a Sabbath day meant a time to put aside the tasks and duties of the other days and to worship God. The Sabbath is meant to be a day of rest, renewal, and refreshment of the spirit.

Yet, for many of us, the Sabbath has become a day like any other, except that we may attend a church service. After that, it's back to the hustle and bustle of work and shopping and catching up on everything that has been neglected the rest of the week: everything, that is, except for the nurturing of our spirits.

Finding Calm in the Chaos incorporates a "Sabbath Celebration" into each week. On this day, set aside time for silence, prayer, and reflection. There are questions for thought and for journaling, if you wish to do this.

Make the Sabbath Celebration a special time. Use a candle that is different from the ordinary: a special candle, perhaps, with an unusual shape or color, or something plain and simple, if that is your style. Find a quiet place where you will not be interrupted. Light the candle, read the Bible passage, sit in silence, and pray. When you are through, place the candle where you can see it during the week as a reminder of the need for Sabbath time, but don't use this candle for anything other than the Sabbath Celebration.

Above all, weave moments of quiet reflection into your day. Write in a journal if that is something that you like to do. Listen to uplifting, spirit-renewing music. Take a walk. Give your time to God.

Many people will choose Sunday as their Sabbath Celebration day. If you work on Sunday but have another day during the week that works better for your Sabbath Celebration, that's fine. The important thing is to find a day each week where you set aside extra time to let the Spirit of God fill your spirit. It is only by filling our own well that we can pour a cup of water for someone else.

Guidelines for a Sabbath Celebration

> God saw everything he had made, and indeed it was very good. And there was evening and there was morning, the sixth day.
>
> Thus the heavens and the earth were finished. And on the seventh day, God finished the work he had done, and he rested on the seventh day from all the work he had done. So God blessed the seventh day and hallowed it, because on it God rested from the work that he had done in creation.
>
> Gen. 1:31–2:3

> Remember the sabbath day, and keep it holy.
>
> Exod. 20:8

Following are some guidelines for creating a Sabbath Celebration.

1. Be conscious of your breathing. Take slow, deep breaths during the day.

2. Use a Breath Prayer. Silently pray the first line as you breathe in, the second line as you breathe out. A different Breath Prayer, based on the Scripture reading, is provided for each week.
3. Allow for times of silence.
4. Light your Sabbath Celebration candle and sit quietly.
5. Read the Bible verse of the week.
6. Use a journal for your reflections.
7. Pray, using the suggestions offered if you wish.

Blessings to you as you seek to find the peace of Christ in the everyday chaos.

Kathleen Long Bostrom
May 2005

JANUARY
CREATION

WEEK 1

DAY 1

Read the following Bible passage each day this week: Genesis 1–2:3. (Read Genesis, chapter 1, from your own Bible; then focus on the following verses from 1:31–2:3.)

> God saw everything that he had made, and indeed, it was very good. And there was evening and there was morning, the sixth day.
>
> Thus the heavens and the earth were finished, and all their multitude. And on the seventh day God finished the work that he had done, and he rested on the seventh day from all the work that he had done. So God blessed the seventh day and hallowed it, because on it God rested from all the work that he had done in creation.

Spirit Booster: Reaching In
God took time each day to stop and celebrate creation. God didn't wait until all the work was done to stop and say, "That's good!" Think of gifts of creation for which you are grateful, and say, "That's good!" (For example: "The sun is shining on the lake this morning. That's good!") Write them down in a journal.

Spirit Booster: Reaching Out

Write a brief note to someone telling that person what you appreciate about him or her. Or call on the phone and tell the person directly. You can write a note to someone in your immediate family, too—it doesn't have to be a person who lives far away. Sometimes it is the people closest to us who need to know that we value them.

Pray for that person each day this week.

☙ ☙

DAY 2
For Goodness' Sake!

How many times does the word "good" appear in the first chapter of Genesis?

God saw that the light was good.
God saw that the waters and land were good.
God saw that the vegetation, plants, trees, and fruit were good.
God saw that the sun and moon and stars were good.
God saw that the creatures of the sea and sky were good.
God saw that the land animals were good.
God saw everything made in those days of creation and proclaimed it all "very good."
God blessed each day with the affirmation that creation was "good."

In what frame of mind do we close each day before we go to sleep?

Can we look at the basics—the sun and stars and lakes and birds—and be thankful? It's so easy to take the basics for granted.

There is such joy indicated in the story of God creating

the world, joy that we sometimes lose in the shuffle because we aren't aware of how glorious every living creature is. (Okay, so flies aren't so glorious, but for the most part. . . .)

God's blessing of each day provides a pattern for how we can close each day:

With an affirmation of the goodness that God provides,

With a sense of joy in the wonders we take for granted,

With gratitude for being created by a God whose first thought is that people are *very good*. Even when we make terrible mistakes, or waste our potential, or fail to appreciate the beautiful world made by God, God knows better. God knows us better than we know ourselves.

For goodness' sake, start a new tradition. Try closing each day with an affirmation of the goodness of God's creation.

Do this—for goodness' sake—and for your own sake, too!

DAY 3
i thank You God

i thank You God for most this amazing
day: for the leaping greenly spirits of trees
and a blue true dream of sky; and for everything
which is natural which is infinite which is yes

(i who have died am alive again today,
and this is the sun's birthday; this is the birth

day of life and of love and wings: and of the gay
great happening illimitably earth)

how should tasting touching hearing seeing
breathing any—lifted from the no
of all nothing—human merely being
doubt unimaginable You?

(now the ears of my ears awake and
now the eyes of my eyes are opened)
—E. E. Cummings, *Complete Poems 1904–1962*, 167

DAY 4

I thank you for the house in which I live,
    For the gray roof on which the raindrops slant;
I thank you for a garden and the slim young shoots
    That mark the old-fashioned things I plant.

I thank you for a daily task to do,
    For books that are my ships with golden wings.
For mighty gifts let others offer praise
    Lord, I am thanking you for little things.
            —Anonymous, *The One Year Book*
              of Personal Prayer, April 12

DAY 5
When God Met Mother Nature

"Is God married to Mother Nature?" five-year-old Cami
asked her father one day. He managed to swallow his smile
and give his daughter an answer that put the relationship
in perfect perspective.

"No, they aren't married," he said to his little girl. "They're just good friends."

God married to Mother Nature, or better yet, just good friends. I cannot imagine a better way of describing God's connection to nature. "God saw everything he had made, and indeed, it was very good" (Gen. 1:31).

Once the creation of the earth was complete, God filled it with plants and animals and every living thing. God then gave people the responsibility to take care of it all. But we haven't done a very good job. Pollution permeates the air, and highways are strewn with trash. Rotting junk heaps and landfills scar the land, and chemicals inject a permanent poison into Mother Nature's tender veins. Bullets and bombs rip open the earth's surface, leaving ragged wounds that never fully heal.

Having dominion over the world does not give us permission to dominate and destroy it. Our power over the earth calls us to protect, nurture, and treasure the beauty of God's creation. It can be as simple as teaching our children not to litter, or cleaning up after your dog when you go for a walk, or using natural methods of pest and weed control. It means extending a little effort to protect our forests and farmlands from overzealous industry, and speaking up for legislation that seeks to preserve the purity of our lakes and oceans.

If we took the friendship between God and Mother Nature seriously, we'd be more careful about how we treat our environment. This world is a precious and marvelous gift, one that should be treated with as much kindness and compassion as we would give a dear and beloved friend.

In anticipation of his upcoming birthday, my youngest son, then five, said to me, "I don't need a birthday present from God. God already gave me a wonderful gift—the whole world!" Would that we all thought that way.

The knowledge that God and Mother Nature are just good friends seemed to sit well with Cami. In fact, she was relieved. Now that Mother Nature is no longer a potential suitor, Cami has put in her bid for God's hand in marriage.

Might as well aim high.

DAY 6

"We have divorced nature from nature's God. We view nature essentially as a toolbox. Nature may have beauty but no purpose. I am convinced that unless in our own minds we re-wed nature to nature's God, we are not going to save our environment. Caution lest we exhaust our natural resources and kill ourselves in the process—that kind of caution is not enough. What we need beyond caution is reverence. What we need beyond practical fears are moral qualms. Unless nature is 're-sanctified' we will never see nature as worthy of ethical considerations similar to those that presently govern human relations."

—William Sloane Coffin, *Credo*, 111

DAY 7

Breath Prayer: Close your eyes; take several slow, deep breaths; then silently pray this breath prayer in rhythm with your breathing. Repeat several times.

Spirit of the living God,
fall afresh on me.

— Light your Sabbath Celebration candle. Sit quietly for five minutes.
— Read the Bible passage for this week: Genesis 1–2:3.
— Quietly reflect on the goodness of God's creation and

the blessing of taking time to rest and let God renew your spirit.

— Reread the items you wrote down for "Spirit Boosters: Reaching In." Give thanks to God for each gift of creation that you named.
— Write down the blessings of your life in a journal.
— Give thanks for the gift of God's creation.

So God blessed the seventh day and hallowed it, because on it God rested from all the work that he had done in creation. (Gen. 2:3)

WEEK 2

DAY 1

Read the following Bible passages each day this week: John 1:1–4; 12–14.

> In the beginning was the Word, and the Word was with God, and the Word was God. He was in the beginning with God. All things came into being through him, and without him not one thing came into being. What has come into being in him was life, and the life was the light of all people. The light shines in the darkness, and the darkness did not overcome it. . . .
>
> But to all who received him, who believed in his name, he gave power to become children of God, who were born, not of blood or of the will of the flesh or of the will of man, but of God.
>
> And the Word became flesh and lived among us, and we have seen his glory, the glory as of a father's only son, full of grace and truth.

Spirit Booster: Reaching In
Write down three things that you do well. Refer often to this list.

How can you be a light to others? A smile, a kind word, a hug? Try to share God's light with someone every day this week.

☙ ☙

DAY 2
Flickers and Flames

I love a cloudy day, dark clouds tumbling through the sky. Maybe in part it's because I grew up in southern California, where such days were few and the meteorological term "scattered showers" meant "scattered throughout the year" rather than throughout the day.

People need different amounts of light. A person with SAD (Seasonal Affective Disorder) feels depressed when the sun isn't shining and is particularly at risk during the winter, when the days are shorter and the intensity of the sunlight diminished. A bright, sunny day can bring profound relief to someone with this condition. On the other side of the spectrum, a person who suffers migraines can barely stand any light at all when in the midst of an episode. Light itself is painful and only serves to magnify the problem.

Different people respond to different amounts—and types—of light. The same applies to our spiritual lives. Some people can stand a great deal of light, the brighter the better, while others are best served by a soft glow. Some of us are comfortable with expressing our faith in bold, exuberant ways, while others express their faith in quiet devotion.

Both flickers and flames are equal in God's sight. We all need to find the most comfortable way to express what we believe. There is no one, correct way. Some prefer florescent light; some do best with candlelight. The source of all light is the same: "What has come into being in him was life, and the life was the light of all people" (John 1:4).

Let your light shine, as a flicker or a flame, and know that whatever shape or size or amount, the light of Christ shines in you.

DAY 3

You are the future,
the red sky before sunrise
over the fields of time.

You are the cock's crow when night is done,
you are the dew and the bells of matins,
maiden, stranger, mother, death.

You create yourself in ever-changing shapes
that rise from the stuff of our days —
unsung, unmourned, undescribed,
like a forest we never knew.

You are the deep innerness of all things,
the last word that can never be spoken.
To each of us you reveal yourself differently:
to the ship as coastline, to the shore as a ship.
                    — Rainer Maria Rilke, *Rilke's Book*
                              of Hours, 119

DAY 4

O thou,
who are the Light of the minds that know Thee,
and the Life of the souls that love Thee,
and the Strength of the thoughts that seek Thee;
help us so to know Thee that we may truly love Thee;
so to love Thee that we may truly serve Thee,
whose service is perfect freedom;
through Jesus Christ our Lord. Amen.
                    —*Gelasian Sacramentary* (6th–8th c.
                                    liturgical book)

DAY 5
Passing the Light

There is a Gaelic tradition known as *grieshog,* a method of passing one day's warmth on to the next. At night, warm coals are buried in ashes. In the morning, the chill quickly dissipates as a fire is made from the buried coals. The process is more than just practical; it is holy as well. With the preservation of warmth and light in the darkness, the truth that "even the darkness cannot put out the light" is made evident on a daily basis.

And that isn't all. The Irish tradition of the *grieshog* is also used to "keep the home fires burning"—literally. When a young person marries, or when a family moves, a hot coal is taken from their fire and passed on to the hearth in the new home. Thus the fire—the light—continues to be shared from place to place, home to home, family to family. The fire that has kept a family warm, cooked their food, and given them light is not put out, but continues to shine in the darkness.

Years ago, when I visited my grandmother, she gave me some iris bulbs, as hers had started to overrun her yard. I planted the bulbs in my own garden where, year after year, the blooming iris made me think of my grandmother in her own home miles from mine. We shared a connection, and it felt good knowing that something that had bloomed in my grandmother's garden was now blooming in mine.

We pass the light. We plant the flowers. And in these small acts of sharing, we pass along the good news of Jesus Christ, the light that shines for all the world to see.

DAY 6

"There is no amount of darkness that can extinguish the inner light. The important thing is not to spend our lives trying to control the environment around us. The task is to control the environment within us."
— Joan Chittester, *Listen with the Heart*, 17

DAY 7

Breath Prayer: Close your eyes; take several slow, deep breaths; then silently pray this breath prayer in rhythm with your breathing. Repeat several times.

Jesus is the light,
the light that never fails.

— Light your Sabbath Celebration candle. Sit quietly for five minutes.
— Read the Bible passage for this week: John 1:1–4; 12–14.

— Quietly reflect on the goodness of God's creation and the blessing of taking time to rest and let God renew your spirit.
— Read aloud the items you wrote down for "Spirit Boosters: Reaching In." Begin by saying, "God, thank you for giving me the gift of . . ."
— Write down the ways that you were God's light to someone this week.
— Pray for those who still walk in darkness, and that God will continue to give you opportunities to share the light of Christ.

"You shall keep the sabbath, because it is holy for you."
(Exod. 31:14)

WEEK 3

DAY 1

Read the following Bible passage each day this week:
Psalm 51:10–12.

> Create in me a clean heart, O God.
>   and put a new and right spirit within me.
> Do not cast me away from your presence,
>   and do not take your holy spirit from me.
> Restore to me the joy of your salvation,
>   and sustain in me a willing spirit.

Spirit Booster: Reaching In
Take time to soak in a hot bubble bath or take a soothing
shower. Place lighted candles on the counters and shelves;
throw some rose petals in the bath; play some quiet, calming music. Restoring and cleansing our outsides can be a
way of restoring and cleansing our insides, too.

Spirit Booster: Reaching Out
Holding a grudge or hanging on to a hurt feeling can be
like a window blind keeping the light of Christ from filter-
ing into your soul. Forgiveness is not easy, but sometimes
being able to let go can feel like opening a window and letting the fresh air back in. If you can't face the person

directly, practice in a private, quiet place, saying, "I forgive you. I forgive you. I forgive you." It doesn't erase the hurt, but it helps let off a bit of steam.

DAY 2
Cleanliness Is Next to Godliness

As I was growing up, Saturday was my favorite day of the week. Not because it was a day off from school (which I loved) or because I could sleep in (which I often did). No, on Saturday my life began anew.

Every Saturday morning, I stripped my bed and washed my sheets and blankets. I dusted, polished, vacuumed, and scoured every square inch of space in my bedroom. Sometimes, just for the change, I rearranged the furniture, no easy feat in a room only eleven feet square in size. By the time I finished, my room could have easily passed the white glove test.

Saturday night, I focused my cleansing zeal upon myself, filing my nails, washing my hair, soaking my brushes and combs so as not to defile my efforts too soon. If cleanliness is next to godliness, I was in line for sainthood.

When the sun slipped between the dark horizon and the waves of the Pacific Ocean, I slipped between my clean sheets and felt complete, renewed, ready to face the rest of the week.

There's something deep within us that longs to be clean, to be renewed, to wash away the dirt and filth that clogs our spiritual pores. We crave to feel scoured down to our very soul. "Create in me a clean heart, O God, and renew a right spirit within me," is the way the psalmist puts it. Help me, O God, to scrub away the guilt, to flush away the regrets, to polish and oil the rusty hinges that constrain my spirit. Help me, O God, to step out of the stagnant waters and to allow the rivers of baptism to flow through my soul.

The apostle Paul writes about the way we can achieve this spiritual cleansing: "So if anyone is in Christ, there is a new creation: everything old has passed away; see, everything has become new!" (2 Cor. 5:17). But it is not our achievement; it is God's: "All this is from God, who reconciled us to himself through Christ" (v. 18). As we confess our sins to God, seek forgiveness, and trust in Christ's undying love, we find our souls swept clean, made new. We've been given the chance to put things right between God and us.

And that is the foundation for putting the rest of our spiritual lives in order. We are new creations in Jesus Christ. We are ambassadors, who share the good news of Jesus with others, in the way we believe and in the way we live.

Like keeping house, caring for our souls takes time and work. It takes time spent in prayer, in reading the Bible, and in quiet thought. It takes work, putting aside our own hurts and disappointments and reaching out to be reconciled with those from whom we are estranged. Tending to the cleansing of our spirits takes a lot more effort than running the vacuum, but it is an effort far more worthy of our time.

I still like the feel of sun-dried sheets, the smell of lemon-oil polish, the shine of a clean-scrubbed floor. I don't experience them as often as I would like. I have children now. And though a clean house is still a priority for me, it is not at the top of my list.

My children are learning how to keep house. They're also learning how to keep their spiritual lives in order. And if I had to choose which one of these tasks I'd rather have them spend their time on, it wouldn't be the one that used a dust rag.

But then again, the rhythm of a mop makes a nice accompaniment to the singing of a hymn.

DAY 3
Why I Wake Early

Hello, sun in my face.
Hello, you who make the morning
and spread it over the fields
and into the faces of the tulips
and the nodding morning glories,
and into the windows of, even, the
miserable and the crotchety—

best preacher that ever was,
dear star, that just happens
to be where you are in the universe
to keep us from ever-darkness,
to ease us with warm touching,
to hold us in the great hands of light—
good morning, good morning, good morning.
—Mary Oliver, *Why I Wake Early*, 3

DAY 4
A Prayer of Daniel (Dan. 9:4–6, 18–19)

"Ah, Lord, great and awesome God, keeping covenant and steadfast love with those who love you and keep your commandments, we have sinned and done wrong, acted wickedly and rebelled, turning aside from your commandments and ordinances. We have not listened to your servants the prophets, who spoke in your name to our kings, our princes, and our ancestors, and to all the people of the land. . . .

We do not present our supplication before you on

the ground of our righteousness, but on the ground of your great mercies. O Lord, hear; O Lord, forgive; O Lord, listen and act and do not delay! For your own sake, O my God, because your city and your people bear your name!"

DAY 5
Out of the Mouths of Babes

"Out of the mouths of babes," it says in Psalm 8, and there is more truth to this than any of us know.

In the early years of our ministry, prior to the arrival of our children, Greg and I loved to ask open-ended questions of the kids during the children's time in worship. We could always count on a few verbal and outgoing tykes to speak up and say anything that came to mind. We could also identify the parents of these loquacious youngsters by the way they would sink down in the pew, shake their blushing faces, or laughingly bury their heads in their hands. "Just you wait!" they would tell us gleefully. "Someday, it will be your children up front, and then we can watch you squirm!"

This prophecy came to pass. Our three children were born within four years, welcomed with much love and affection on the part of the whole congregation. It wasn't long before our oldest, Christopher, joined the rest of the younger folks on the steps of the chancel, delighting one and all as he spontaneously gave Greg and me each an affectionate hug after the closing prayer. And he always had something to say, relevant or not. The parents who had suffered through their own children's orations a few years before now sat smugly in the pews, grinning with justified and loving revenge as we tried to keep our young son in check.

One Sunday morning during the children's time, Greg was explaining the proximity of God. "Where is God? Is God in this church? Is God in the sky?" he asked. Several children raised their hands, offering suggestions. Then it was Christopher's turn. His hand lifted high, he would not lower it until Greg reluctantly called his name.

With pure sincerity, Christopher looked up at his father, his brown velvet eyes seeing beyond time and place. "I have always believed," he said, with the accumulated knowledge of a five-year-old, and all the wisdom of the ages, "that the whole world was in God's heart."

The church was hushed. "Let us pray," Greg said, and we all bowed our heads. Nothing else needed to be said.

DAY 6

"God, grant me the serenity to accept the things I cannot change, the courage to change the things I can, and the wisdom to know the difference."
— Reinhold Niebuhr, *The Westminster Collection of Christian Quotations,* 2

DAY 7

Breath Prayer: Close your eyes; take several slow, deep breaths; then silently pray this breath prayer in rhythm with your breathing. Repeat several times.

Create in me a clean heart, O God;
put a new and right spirit within me.

- Light your Sabbath Celebration candle. Sit quietly for five minutes.
- Read the Bible passage for this week: Psalm 51:10–12.
- Quietly reflect on the power of God to cleanse your heart of the grime that keeps you from fully loving, and think about all the obstacles that keep you from allowing the love of Christ to renew your spirit.
- For what do you need to be forgiven? Whom do you need to forgive? Tell God, and don't feel pressured to forgive unless you truly sense that you are ready to do so.
- Write down the times that you have been forgiven, by someone else or by God. Think about how you felt when you were forgiven.
- Pray for those who have hurt you, or against whom you have a grudge, that God will help you forgive and be forgiven.

The word "Sabbath" comes from the Hebrew word "Shabbat" which means "to rest."

WEEK 4

DAY 1

Read the following Bible passage each day this week: 2 Corinthians 5:17–20.

> So if anyone is in Christ, there is a new creation: everything old has passed away; see, everything has become new! All this is from God, who reconciled us to himself through Christ, and has given us the ministry of reconciliation; that is, in Christ God was reconciling the world to himself, not counting their trespasses against them, and entrusting the message of reconciliation to us. So we are ambassadors for Christ, since God is making his appeal through us; we entreat you on behalf of Christ, be reconciled to God.

Spirit Booster: Reaching In
It is easy to forget to breathe: pain, stress, and worry all cause us to take shallow breaths, and even to hold our breath. Practice deep breathing by placing your hand on your abdomen and breathing in slowly, then out. When you catch yourself in a tense moment, stop and breathe!

Spirit Booster: Reaching Out
The next time you get a phone call from a charity wanting you to donate used items, think about how nice it would be to be the person on the other end, receiving something new instead of used. Buy a new article of clothing and give it away, as a way of representing that you are made new in Christ!

⚭

DAY 2
Mental Millinery

I'm not one of those people who dawdle away the morning in their pajamas. No sooner do my feet hit the floor than I'm pulling on my clothes for the day. I choose my wardrobe carefully, in preparation for the tasks that await me. The most important item of clothing comes from my collection of hats.

These are no ordinary hats, mind you. They hang upon a wall that exists only in my imagination, yet they are as real to me as the shoes and dresses and shirts that clutter my closet. They are the hats that shape my life.

They come in all shapes, sizes, and colors. Big hats and little hats. Working hats, play hats. Bright, crisp, new hats and worn, tattered, old hats. Some of them I picked out myself. Others I have received as gifts. It has been a long time since I went without one.

What hat shall I wear today? Do I choose the wool shepherd's hat of ministry? It has the magical ability to change from a scholarly shape to a more relaxed, pastoral appearance as the need arises. I could try the wide-brimmed, straw gardener's hat and plant those flowers that are still sitting in their original pots. The hat I'd like to put on is the thinking cap, the one I wear when I write, but I'm not sure I have time today. I ought to see if the ancient dust cap still fits—it's been awhile since I wore it, and the condition of my house attests to that fact. The swim cap looks enticing. A few laps in the pool might be a good way to start the day.

I reach up and feel the functional, food-stained hat of motherhood still in place. It never comes off for long. There's the occasional moment when I remove it so my scalp can breathe, like late at night when everyone is tucked into bed and I sit, sip tea, and read. Even then, the hat lies within reach. I know I will continue to wear it even long after my children have grown. Sometimes I find it restricting, getting in the way of others I'd like to wear. Still, it's the hat I cherish most.

Hanging in the shadows, the baby bonnet is starting to yellow. It reminds me that I am a daughter, blessed by two loving parents. With my mother gone and my father living many miles away, this bonnet is even more precious to me. There's the wedding veil, worn twenty-four years ago. It too often gets lost in the shuffle of all the other hats. The lace on it is delicate but strong. I'm looking forward to seeing how it looks when it's fifty years old.

Most days I wear a variety of hats, some in succession, some simultaneously. They don't always go together very well. I pull and tug and force them on anyway. When my head starts to throb, I know I've put on too many, or that one needs a little readjustment. My body has a way of telling me when my hats get out of hand. I listen as best I can.

I haven't had a chance to wear some hats yet. I'm anxious to find out what they might be. A poet's beret? A grandmother's hat? I'll know when the time comes to put them on.

It is time to make my daily selection. I stretch out my arm, then let it drop. I think I'll try going without a hat today, just to see what happens. I open the door and step outside. A frisky breeze skips through my hair.

Every day, I am a new creation in Christ.

DAY 3

Finish then thy New Creation,
  Pure and spotless let us be;
Let us see thy great salvation
  Perfectly restored in thee,
Changed from glory into glory
  Till in heaven we take our place,
Till we cast our crowns before thee,
  Lost in wonder, love, and praise!
— Charles Wesley, *The Westminster
    Collection of Christian
    Quotations*, 166

DAY 4
Our true home

God before and God behind,
God for us and God for your own self,
  Maker of heaven and earth,
  creator of sea and sky,
  governor of day and night.
We give thanks for your ordered gift of life to us,
  for the rhythms that reassure,
  for the equilibriums that sustain,
  for the reliabilities that curb our anxieties.
    We treasure from you,
      days to work and nights to rest.
    We cherish from you,
      days to control and nights to yield.
    We savor from you,
      days to plan and nights to dream.

Be our day and our night,
  our heaven and our earth,
  our sea and our sky,
    and in the end our true home. Amen.
        —Walter Brueggemann, *Awed to Heaven,*
                Rooted in Earth, 21

DAY 5
The Bells of Ou Dong

I came across a small index card that I have kept in my files for thirty years or more. It tells the story of the Korean city of Ou Dong. Attached to the card is a small, metal bell.

Long after the Korean war, the ravages of destruction remain embedded in the land. Scattered across the earth are broken shell casings, leftovers from bullets and bombs. They are ever-present reminders of the horrors that took place, these fragments of violence.

The people of Ou Dong have turned the scraps of metal into something life-giving. Children scour the fields, glean the sharp pieces from the soft earth, and take them to small cottage foundries, where the metal is melted and then recast as small bells. The bells are used to trim the harnesses of the oxen that plow the fields and carry the loads and are the indispensable cornerstone of life in this agricultural region.

The people who have known the terrors of war have found a way to redeem the horrors and transform them into a better way of life.

Shells into bells. Death into life. The old has passed away. Behold, the new has come.

DAY 6

"Creation, then, is an ongoing story of new beginnings, opportunities to begin again and again."
— Wayne Muller, *Sabbath*, 36

DAY 7

Breath Prayer: Close your eyes; take several slow, deep breaths; then silently pray this breath prayer in rhythm with your breathing. Repeat several times.

In Christ, I am a new creation;
the old has passed away!

— Light your Sabbath Celebration candle. Sit quietly for five minutes.
— Read the Bible passage for this week: 2 Corinthians 5:17–20.
— You are a new creation in Christ! Repeat that thought several times: "In Christ, I am a new creation!" Allow that truth to sink into your soul.
— Is there some way in which you need to be reconciled to God? To yourself? To someone else?
— What are the "old things" of your life that you need to hand over to God so that they can pass away?
— Pray for each day to be a new creation, and for reconciliation to happen in your life and in the world.

"Come to me, all you that are weary and are carrying
heavy burdens, and I will give you rest." (Matt. 11:28)

FEBRUARY
LOVE

WEEK 1

DAY 1

Read the following Bible passage each day this week:
Micah 6:8.

> He has told you, O mortal, what is good:
>   and what does the Lord require of you
> but to do justice, and to love kindness,
>   and to walk humbly with your God?

Spirit Booster: Reaching In
Recall a time when someone blessed you with an act of
kindness. How did that feel? Cherish that act of kindness
in and of itself without feeling obligated to justify or
return it.

Spirit Booster: Reaching Out
If you regularly support a particular charity, pray each day
for that charity and the people it serves. You may wish to
investigate information on other worthwhile charities and
do the same.

DAY 2
Micah's "To Do" List

Sounds so simple, doesn't it?

"Do justice. Love kindness. Walk humbly with your God."

Almost sounds like one of the many "to do" lists we tack up on our refrigerators. "Hmmm . . . what do I need to do today? Pick up the dry cleaning. Buy a birthday card for Uncle Ed. Take the cat to the vet for her shots. Oh, yes — and do justice, love kindness, and walk humbly with God."

Guess which chores get checked off the list? Most likely, justice, kindness, and walking humbly get put off until another day. There may be time to walk the dog and walk on the treadmill, but walking humbly with God? Maybe some other time.

Interesting that Micah listed these three requirements as verbs. If we want to be people of faith, we are *to do* justice, *to love* kindness, *to walk* humbly with our God. "To do," "to love," and "to walk" imply action on our part. It isn't just a matter of *being* a just person, but *doing* acts of justice; it's not enough to *be* a kind person if you aren't *doing* kindness. As for walking with God, the word "walk" implies that there is an action taking place. Don't just sit on your faith; get up and go somewhere with it!

Along with being verbs of action, these three requirements are inextricably linked. In this way, one must do justice in order to love kindness in order to walk humbly with God. The order can be reversed, too. If you walk humbly with God, you are bound to do acts of kindness, which in turn bring about instances of justice.

Micah leaves the door wide open for how we are "to do" these requirements. We each must decide exactly how we intend to flesh them out.

Perhaps writing them all down on our "to do" list, keeping them at the top of that list, and never checking them off is a good way to start.

DAY 3
Transaction

What is it that God requires?
    We aspire
        God's desire.
Shall we aim for something higher?
    Let's inquire:

    Just to *love*
    to *do*
    to *be*.
Verbs, all three.

Here there is an action faction.
    No abstraction.
        Interaction.

God inspires:
    We acquire.
    Jesus, set our hearts on fire.

DAY 4

Kindle, O Lord, in our hearts, we pray,
the flame of that love which never ceases
that it may burn in us and give light to others.

May we shine forever in your temple,
set on fire with that eternal light of yours
which puts to flight the darkness of this world;
in the name of Jesus Christ your Son our Lord.
— Source unknown, *The Complete Book
of Christian Prayer*, 59

DAY 5
Did You Say *Justice*?

". . . with liberty and justice for all."

I remember an essay contest sponsored by my elementary school when I was in fourth or fifth grade. Our challenge was to put the "Pledge of Allegiance" into our own words, to open up the meaning in what I know now was an attempt to make us think about what we said every day. I remember *not* winning the contest, but that wasn't a big surprise to me. As I wrote my essay, I realized with some astonishment that the words I repeated each school morning, with my hand placed dutifully across my heart, were words whose meaning I didn't fully understand and rarely thought about. Concepts such as "pledge," "allegiance," "indivisible." Words worth thinking about. Maybe the best definitions aren't the ones we find in the dictionary.

My friend's preschool daughter came home from school one day. She proudly began to recite the words of the "Pledge of Allegiance" for her mother. She rattled off the words, just as the rest of us have for so many years. As her recitation came to a conclusion, the words that came tumbling out of little Elizabeth's mouth caught her mother off guard.

". . . with liberty and juice box for all."

"Not a bad take on it," my friend said. "Sometimes justice really does mean juice boxes—and lunches to go with them—for all."

I think the prophet Micah might agree with that.

DAY 6

"And this more human love (that will fulfill itself, infinitely considerate and gentle, and kind and clear in binding and releasing) will resemble that which we are preparing with struggle and toil, the love that consists in this, that two solitudes protect and border and salute each other."
—Rainer Maria Rilke, *Letters to a Young Poet*, 59

DAY 7

Breath Prayer: Close your eyes; take several slow, deep breaths; then silently pray this breath prayer in rhythm with your breathing. Repeat several times.

Allow me, O God,
to walk humbly with you.

— Light your Sabbath Celebration candle. Sit quietly for five minutes.
— Read the Bible passage for this week: Micah 6:8.
— Quietly reflect on the three things God requires of you: to do justice, to love kindness, and to walk humbly with God.
— Repeat several times: "Do justice. Love kindness. Walk humbly." Print these words on a card and put the card somewhere where you will see it every day.

— In your journal, write down a kindness that someone has done for you.
— Pray for charities and the work they do, and for the people they serve.

"Give liberally and be ungrudging when you do so, for on this account the LORD your God will bless you in all your work." (Deut. 15:10)

WEEK 2

DAY 1

Read the following Bible passage each day this week:
Mark 12:28–31.

> One of the scribes came near and heard them dis-
> puting with one another, and seeing that [Jesus]
> answered them well, he asked him, "Which com-
> mandment is the first of all?" Jesus answered, "The
> first is, 'Hear, O Israel: the Lord our God, the Lord
> is one; you shall love the Lord your God with all
> your heart, and with all your soul, and with all your
> mind, and with all your strength.' The second is
> this, 'You shall love your neighbor as yourself.'"
> There is no other commandment greater than
> these.

Spirit Booster: Reaching In
This Bible passage states clearly that we are to love our
neighbors as ourselves. What do you love about yourself?
If you find it difficult to think in these terms, remember
that since we are created in God's image, there are good
qualities to be found in every person!

Spirit Booster: Reaching Out
Find time to compliment your neighbors, whether that means telling them how glad you are to have them as neighbors, what a beautiful yard they have, or something similar. Or, do an "invisible good deed" by taking the newspaper to your neighbors' front door, bringing them their mail, or offering to help with yard work.

DAY 2
Publish or Perish

My two sons sat in a warm tub of water, scrubbing their knees and chatting together.

"David, do you want to be a scientist when you grow up?" asked Christopher, then eight.

"No," replied David, my youngest son, with a serious note in his voice. "I'm going to be a publisher and publish Mommy's books."

It took me four years of trying before I had my first book accepted for publication. My children suffered through this time with me, as I agonized over continuous rejection letters yet still kept trying to get published. One year Christopher told Santa that what he wanted most for Christmas was for Mommy to get a book published. I think David was tired of waiting on Santa and so decided to take matters into his own hands.

What touched my heart the most about this bath-time dialogue was David's keen sense of my heart's desire. He hadn't the slightest idea what a publisher was, but that didn't matter. He loved his Mommy and wanted to make me happy, even if it meant devoting his life to the cause.

As children of God, shouldn't our goal be similar? To be so in touch with God's true desire that we dedicate our lives to making that a reality? What is it that God wants?

A man asked Jesus this question once, in somewhat different words, "Which commandment is the first of all?" And Jesus answered, "You shall love the Lord your God with all your heart, and with all your soul, and with all your mind, and with all your strength" (Mark 12:30). That certainly covers all the bases.

Living as Christ wishes us to live is a tall order. It is a lifelong task. It seems at times as far from our reach as my ever getting published was. But because of our love for Christ, we seek with joy. The Christian life demands no less than the giving of our whole selves to the one who gave his life for us.

DAY 3
You Shall

YOU.
You SHALL.
    You shall LOVE.
    You shall love the Lord
    your God
With ALL:
    with all your heart
  and with *all*
    with all your soul
  and with *all*
    with all your mind
  and with *all*
    with all your strength
and
    and
    AND
    your neighbor as

yourself
your . . . self.
YOU.
You SHALL.
You shall LOVE.

DAY 4

Eternal goodness,
you want me to gaze into you
and see that you love me.
You love me freely,
and you want me
to love and serve my neighbours
with the same love,
offering them my prayers and my possessions,
as far as in me lies.
O God, come to my assistance!
—St. Catherine of Siena, *The Book of a Thousand Prayers*, 50

DAY 5
The Best Lesson of the Day

It was a good morning at church. Everything had run smoothly for the first day of Sunday School. The children and adults found their classrooms with little confusion. The two new worship times brought in a fine attendance. I shook hands at the door, hung up my clerical robe, and gathered a happy flock of children, two of my own plus some friends who planned to spend the afternoon at our house.

As morning slipped easily into afternoon, the well-ordered day turned to chaos. Just before we left the church, I spotted a church member standing nearby with a couple of strangers: a middle-aged man and his adolescent son. They needed a place to stay, they said. They had no money, no food. Could we help?

I couldn't just walk away. I offered to see what I could do.

Half an hour and numerous telephone calls later, I finally reached someone who thought they might be able to offer a night's shelter. I struggled to hear the voice on the other end of the line while at the same time trying to attend to the children who ran in and out of my office with various complaints.

Another hour passed as I played telephone tag with several volunteers, looking for a place to send this family. Finally, the right contacts were made. I gave the necessary information to the man and his son, then faced my brood of hungry and unhappy children.

As the kids piled into the car, I could tell that they were miffed at the long wait. "You wasted our play time!" one of them declared. "What took you so long?" another demanded. Rather than get defensive and angry, or start to cry (a serious option at that point), I told them why we had been delayed. A family needed help. They had no home, no food. I had been trying to find a way the church could do something to help.

The children's indignation instantly turned to concern. "We can collect our money," one suggested. "Let's give them some of our clothes," said another. "How about we take them out to eat?" a third responded. Despite my frayed nerves and fatigue, a smile warmed my face as I listened to the children trying to live their Christian faith, to love their neighbor as Christ calls us to do.

It was a good morning at church. But I have to admit, the best lesson of the day came later.

DAY 6

So, friends, every day do something
that won't compute. Love the Lord.
Love the world. Work for nothing.
Take all that you have and be poor.
Love someone who does not deserve it.
. . . .
Practice resurrection.

> —Wendell Berry, excerpts from
> "Manifesto," in *Collected Poems,*
> *1957–1982,* 151–52

DAY 7

Breath Prayer: Close your eyes; take several slow, deep
breaths; then silently pray this breath prayer in rhythm
with your breathing. Repeat several times.

> *The Lord my God . . .*
> *The Lord is one.*

— Light your Sabbath Celebration candle. Sit quietly for
  five minutes.
— Read the Bible passage for this week: Mark 12:28–31.
— Quietly reflect on how God's commandment is all about
  love: love God, love neighbor, love self.
— How do you love God with your heart? With your soul?
  With your mind? With your strength? Try to clarify
  what is meant by "heart," "soul," "mind," and "strength,"

and use each word in a sentence. For example: "I love God with all the deepest feelings I have (heart)."

— In your journal, write down all the words that come to mind when you think of the ways that you love God.
— Use the prayers from this week, and don't forgot to tell God, "I love you."

The seventh day is a Sabbath to the Lord your God.
(Exod. 20:10)

WEEK 3

DAY 1

Read the following Bible passage each day this week:
Psalm 86:1–7.

> Incline your ear, O LORD, and answer me,
>   for I am poor and needy.
> Preserve my life, for I am devoted to you;
>   save your servant who trusts in you.
> You are my God; be gracious to me, O Lord,
>   for to you do I cry all day long.
> Gladden the soul of your servant,
>   for to you, O Lord, I lift up my soul.
> For you, O Lord, are good and forgiving,
>   abounding in steadfast love to all who call on you.

Spirit Booster: Reaching In
Personalize the psalm by substituting your name for the
pronouns "me" and "I." (Example: "Incline your ear, O
Lord, and answer Kathy, for Kathy is poor and needy.")

Spirit Booster: Reaching Out
The news is always full of stories of people in crisis. Scan
the newspaper or listen to the news and pray for someone
you don't know who is in need. As you did in "Reaching

In," substitute that person's name wherever you find the pronouns "me" and "I" and use this as a prayer.

◌◌◌◌

DAY 2
God's Inclination

"Incline your ear, O Lord, and answer me" is the way the New Revised Standard Version begins Psalm 86.

The New Living Translation writes, "Bend down, O Lord, and hear my prayer." In the King James Version, the opening line is "Bow down thine ear, O Lord, hear me."

Incline. Bend down. Bow down. All of these convey the image of God drawing close to the one who is praying, turning God's ear toward the person who cries out in need. It is a tender, gentle, loving image. It reminds me of a parent kneeling down to a child's level and drawing close to that child in a physical gesture that says, "Right now, what you have to say to me is the most important thing in the world."

In church on Sunday, during the children's time, as the chancel area filled with noisy, chattering children, one mother sat in the front pew holding her two-year-old, who was somewhat intimidated by all the people and commotion. The little girl wanted to say something to her mother, and her mother tilted her head to the little girl's face so that the child could whisper in her ear. I sat next to them, watching. I couldn't hear what the child said, and I wasn't meant to hear it. But I saw the mother's face light up in a smile as she listened. Once the child said what she needed to say, she snuggled down into her mother's arms, content and safe.

When we are intimidated by the world, or overwhelmed by some sorrow or concern, God bends down, bows down, and inclines that heavenly ear to us, so that we can whisper our prayer and trust that we are heard. When we pray out of a sincere heart, God holds us close and listens and says to us, "Right now, what you have to say to me is the most important thing in the world."

"Incline your ear, O Lord, and answer me. Bend down, bow down, and hear me."

And now, O God, let me do the same for you.

DAY 3
Love Bade Me Welcome

Love bade me welcome; yet my soul drew back,
    Guilty of dust and sin.
But quick-eyed Love, observing me grow slack
    From my first entrance in,
Drew nearer to me, sweetly questioning
    If I lacked any thing.

"A guest," I answered, "worthy to be here";
    Love said, "You shall be he."
"I the unkind, ungrateful? Ah my dear,
    I cannot look on Thee."
Love took my hand, and smiling did reply,
    "Who made the eyes but I?"

"Truth Lord, but I have marred them: let my shame
    Go where it doth deserve."
"And know you not," says Love, "who bore the blame?"
    "My dear, then I will serve."
"You must sit down," says Love, "and taste My meat."
    So I did sit and eat.
      —George Herbert, *The Complete English Works*, 184

DAY 4

Give me, good Lord, a full faith, a firm hope, and a
    fervent charity, a love of you incomparably above the
    love of myself.
Give me, good Lord, a longing to be with you, not to avoid
    the calamities of this world, not so much to attain the
    joys of heaven, as simply for love of you.
                        —Thomas More, *The One Year Book of
                        Personal Prayer,* January 7

∞

DAY 5
How Are You?

How many times have you been asked the question, "How
are you?" It's become a common comment, so common in
fact that often it has little or no meaning except as a means
of being polite. I say it to people all the time, so I'm not
criticizing anyone any more than I am criticizing myself.

There are times when I simply respond, "Fine," because
there is really no time to answer properly. If I did, my
answer would often be, "How am I? You really want to
know? Well, I'll tell you. I am in pain every day. I feel fraz-
zled. My body doesn't work right. I feel like a terrible
mother. I'm not doing the work I should at church. I still
grieve for my mother. I want to be an armadillo and just
curl up and sleep. Oh—and by the way, how are *you?*"

I worked with someone years ago who always asked
me, "How are you?" but never really heard my answer
(which was usually "Okay"). So one day I decided to see
if he actually listened. When he asked me, I replied, "Terrible. The kids are so sick, and I feel buried alive." To

which he responded cheerfully, "That's great!" I hope that he really didn't hear me and was just offering his usual response. Now that I think about it, maybe he *did* hear me. . . .

A friend's uncle is learning Spanish. Never mind that he is in his eighties and mostly blind. He has taken on this challenge with a joyful spirit, which is the way to take on challenges. In a letter to my friend, he told her that one of the responses given colloquially to the common greeting *"Como estas?"* ("How are you?") is *"Aqui en la lucha,"* which means "Here in the struggle." I love that! What a perfect—and honest—answer. So much better than "Fine" when you aren't fine. When there is little time to answer, and you really don't feel like rattling off your litany of personal woes, answering "Here in the struggle" removes both the usual dishonest answers and the self-pitying ones.

In so many psalms—Psalm 86 included—the writer is struggling and pleading to be heard. "God, are you there? Are you listening? Answer me!"

And God says, *"Aqui en la lucha."*

Here in the struggle.

Count on it.

DAY 6

"Of all powers, love is the most powerful and the most powerless. It is the most powerful because it alone can conquer that final and most impregnable stronghold which is the human heart. It is the most powerless because it can do nothing except by consent."
—Frederick Buechner, *Wishful Thinking,* 53–54

DAY 7

Breath Prayer: Close your eyes; take several slow, deep breaths; then silently pray this breath prayer in rhythm with your breathing. Repeat several times.

Incline your ear . . .
and answer me.

— Light your Sabbath Celebration candle. Sit quietly for five minutes.
— Read the Bible passage for this week: Psalm 86:1–7.
— Quietly reflect on God's faithfulness in listening to us when we cry out for help.
— God answers our prayers, even when it is not easy to recognize the answers. Think back on the last year and try to remember prayers you have prayed for which you believe that you have received answers.
— In your journal, write down prayer requests that you would like answered.
— Pray that God will not only listen to you and answer your prayers but that you will be more attentive to listening to God and answering God's requests of you.

Devote yourselves to prayer, keeping alert in it with thanksgiving. (Col. 4:2)

WEEK 4

DAY 1

Read the following Bible passage each day this week: 1 John 4:16–18.

> God is love, and those who abide in love abide in God, and God abides in them. Love has been perfected among us in this: that we may have boldness on the day of judgment, because as he is, so are we in this world. There is no fear in love, but perfect love casts out fear; for fear has to do with punishment, and whoever fears has not reached perfection in love.

Spirit Booster: Reaching In
It is helpful to name our fears so that we can face them and not let them have as much control over us. Name one fear that troubles you and then offer it to God. Use the image of casting a fishing pole, throwing the fear out into the waters and letting God carry it away.

Spirit Booster: Reaching Out
Pray for those who live in fear. Is there someone you know? If so, call or send a note of encouragement.

DAY 2
Take a Vow!

My husband and I are copastors of the same church. Often, we get asked to officiate at weddings together. We always like to tell people that we have "the best seat in the house" because we can see the faces of the bride and groom, with the faces of all their friends and family in the pews behind them.

I always find my own wedding vows renewed when I officiate at a wedding. I think of how the bride and groom stand up in front of God and their family and friends and promise the impossible: to cherish each other every day, always to be faithful, to love the other person for as long as they both shall live. Impossible—but possible because of the love God has given to us in Jesus Christ.

The vows two people make to one another in their wedding are really the vows God makes to us. To love and cherish us forever. Always to be faithful. To be with us in good times and in bad. I began to imagine the traditional wedding vows being vows made between God and all of God's people:

> "I, God, take you, _____,
> To be my child.
> And I promise and covenant
> Before all of heaven and earth,
> To be your loving and faithful God;
> In joy and in sorrow,
> In plenty and in want,
> In sickness and in health,
> As long as you shall live on this earth,
> And forever in the life to come."

And then our response:

"I, _____, take you, Creator of all of life,
To be my loving and faithful God.
And I promise and covenant,
Before you and all of creation,
To be your loving and faithful child;
In joy and in sorrow,
In plenty and in want,
In sickness and in health,
As long as I shall live on this earth,
And forever in the life to come."

For God is love, and those who abide in love abide in God,
and God abides in them.

DAY 3
Perfect Love

Perfect love.
What's that?
   Love that never complains
      when asked to forgive
      the hurts inflicted with intention?

   Or love that keeps its mouth shut
      when feelings are wounded
      and left to bleed?

   Or love that locks the door of the heart
      because there is no room
      for more pain and sorrow?

No! These are not perfect,
and they are not love.

Perfect love
   is love that says "Forgive them"
      when we do not even know what we have done
      and when we do.

Perfect love
   is love that bleeds,
      and seeps into the crevices
      of splintered wood.

Perfect love
   is love that offers open arms
      and only asks that we find room
      in the inn of our soul.

DAY 4

O God of love, we ask you to give us love;
Love in our thinking, love in our speaking,
Love in our doing,
And love in the hidden places of our souls;
Love of those with whom we find it hard to bear,
And love of those who find it hard to bear with us;
Love of those with whom we work,
And love of those with whom we take our ease;
That so at length we may be worthy to dwell with you,
Who are eternal love.
   —William Temple, *The Book of a Thousand Prayers*, 52

DAY 5
Getting a Handle on Fear

Fear is a good thing, right?

It stops you from running out into the middle of the street, for fear of a car racing past.

It keeps you from canceling your checkup with the doctor when you feel that lump in your breast, for fear of what that lump could be.

It causes you to speak out to a group of politicians at your local school, for fear that if you don't, your child's education will be compromised.

Fear can motivate us to do what is right.

Fear can be immobilizing, too.

It stops you from driving to the city to see the collection of Van Gogh's, for fear of the highways and traffic.

It keeps you from getting that medical test done, for fear of what it might show.

It causes you to keep your mouth shut when you want to speak up, for fear of being the only one who feels as you do.

Fear is a motivator. Fear is an inhibitor. Fear is impossible to avoid. And that becomes a problem when fear is associated with faith. As in "If you just have faith, there's nothing for you to fear" and "If you are afraid, your faith isn't strong enough."

I wrestle with the relationship between fear and faith when I read passages from the Bible such as 1 John 4:18: "There is no fear in love, but perfect love casts out fear." That seems to imply that if my faith in and love for God are perfect, then I will have no fear—at all.

But reading these words again in the context of 1 John 4 help to clarify what perfect love really is.

Verse 16 says that "God is love." And God alone is perfect. So, perfect + love = God.

Now, that makes sense.

God casts out fear. The love of God in Jesus Christ casts out fear. It's not that fear is erased from the face of the earth or from the depth of our hearts; it's just that when we do have fear, God is the only one who can get rid of it.

When I sit in the doctor's office waiting to get the results of my mammogram, worried that the lump I feel is going to be the same cancer that took my aunt's life, God is right there with me. No matter what the mammogram shows, God is going to stay right there with me. I hand my fear to God, because it's too much for me to hold. It isn't too much for God.

Anytime we are immobilized by fear, inhibited by fear, or captured by fear, God holds out those beautiful, holy, hole-pierced, whole hands and says, "Hand it over, kiddo. You have enough on your plate right now."

Hand your fear to God. Don't you worry. God can *hand*le it just fine.

DAY 6

"Love involves nourishing someone else's soul and not only finding someone willing to nourish yours."
 —Harold Kushner, *Living a Life That Matters*, 113

DAY 7

Breath Prayer: Close your eyes; take several slow, deep breaths; then silently pray this breath prayer in rhythm with your breathing. Repeat several times.

There is no fear . . .
in perfect love.

— Light your Sabbath Celebration candle. Sit quietly for five minutes.
— Read the Bible passage for this week: 1 John 4:16–18.
— Quietly reflect on what it means to have "perfect love." Think of some instances when the love of another person or of God gave you the courage to overcome your fear.
— Write down in your journal some examples of this.
— Offer to God your fears, and pray for enough love to help you face your fears and be rid of them. Ask God to help you be a person who does not instill fear in others, but rather love.

Celebrating the Sabbath is different from running away. We do not merely leave . . . we actually cease letting them have a hold on our lives. (Marva Dawn, 48)

MARCH
ENDURANCE

WEEK 1

DAY 1

Read the following Bible passage each day this week: Proverbs 6:20–22.

My child, keep your father's commandment,
  and do not forsake your mother's teaching.
Bind them upon your heart always;
  tie them around your neck.
When you walk, they will lead you;
  when you lie down, they will watch over you;
  and when you awake, they will talk with you.
For the commandment is a lamp and the teaching a light.

Spirit Booster: Reaching In
Place a small candle next to your alarm clock (if you use one) or on a table or nightstand near your bed to remind you that, when you go to sleep and when you awake, God's commandment is a lamp and a light in your life.

Spirit Booster: Reaching Out
If you are blessed to have parents who are still living and who are a loving presence in your life, call and tell them. If you do not have living parents, or if your parents were not a positive influence in your life, call someone who has

served as a "father figure" or "mother figure" to you and say how blessed you feel to know that person.

∞ ∞

DAY 2
And I Shall Wake to See the Light

Although I did not grow up attending church, our family still practiced rituals of grace at mealtime and prayers before bed.

My mother taught us this old, childhood prayer: "Now I lay me down to sleep, I pray the Lord my soul to keep. If I shall die before I wake, I pray the Lord my soul to take." However, she did not like the lines about dying in one's sleep, because she felt that was a frightening thought for a child just about to drift off to dreamland. So Mom changed the last two lines:

> And I shall wake to see the light,
> For God is with me all the night.

A much more comforting image, I heartily agree.

The night before my mother died of lung cancer, my father, brother, sister, and I kept vigil by her hospital bed. In the morning, without waking, she took her last breath. I thought about the lines from the prayer that she had taught us all those years before. God indeed was with us all through that long, dark, terrible, holy, and blessed night. And when my mother woke and opened her eyes the morning of March 30, 2000, she did not wake to the harsh florescent hospital lights. She woke in the presence of the Light of the World.

Thank you, Mom, for your teaching, which I hold in my heart; for the loving prayer that is with me wherever I go; and for the words which are a lamp and a light that will always be with me:

Now I lay me down to sleep,
I pray the Lord my soul to keep.
And I shall wake to see the light,
For God is with me all the night.

DAY 3
Into This Silent Night

Into this silent night
   as we make our weary way
      we know not where,
   just when the night becomes its darkest
      and we cannot see our path,
   just then
      is when the angels rush in,
         their hands full of stars.
—Ann Weems, *Kneeling in Bethlehem*, 52

DAY 4

Lord God, I am no longer my own, but yours.
Put me to what you will,
rank me with whom you will.
Put me to doing, put me to enduring;
let me be employed for you,
or laid aside for you,
exalted for you
or brought low for you;
let me be full, let me be empty;
let me have all things,
let me have nothing.
I freely and wholeheartedly yield all things

to your pleasure and disposal.
And now, glorious and blessed God,
Father, Son and Holy Spirit,
you are mine and I am yours.
So be it.

—John Wesley, *The Book of a
Thousand Prayers*, 24

DAY 5
Spelling Bee

Watching your child compete in a spelling bee is a unique form of parental torture. Our eldest son represented his elementary school class in the spelling competition on a yearly basis.

Instead of hearing the *drip drip drip* of water torture, my husband and I endured the agony of listening to *letter letter letter* as Chris and the rest of the students spelled out their words, waiting for the dreaded response from the judge, "Sorry, that is incorrect," that knocked the kids off the stage one by one. It's a situation where a parent roots for every child, because nobody with a heart wants to see anyone lose.

One year, prior to the spelling bee, I jotted a quick note on a piece of paper: "You can do it, Chris. I'm behind you all the way." "Put this in your pocket and read it before the contest," I told him. As Greg and I sat in the audience later that morning, I felt that at least I had given some words of encouragement, to offset the words of trickery that would be hurled at him as he stood before the auditorium of anxious contestants and nervous parents.

Chris made it through the first few rounds, then missed a word. He walked off the stage, and we ached for him from afar. I didn't know if my little note had been a help or not. He didn't say much when we saw him for a few minutes after the spelling bee concluded.

I spent the rest of the day working on a presentation I had to give at a large gathering in another city the next morning. I can preach in front of my own congregation, but when it comes to standing before a live audience of strangers, my nerves kick up. I could relate a bit to what my son must have felt standing on the stage in the school auditorium. I hadn't done much public speaking then (except for preaching) and still felt unsure of my abilities. Surely, the people who had invited me to speak would quickly discover what a fraud I was. As soon as I opened my mouth, the floor on the stage would open and I would drop through the trap doors in humiliation.

The next day, before anyone else was awake, I drove to the conference where I was to speak. I waited nervously in a side room and pulled my speech out of my notebook so I could read it over a few more times.

A scrap of paper dropped to the floor. I picked it up, and there, in my son's handwriting, were these words: "You can do it, Mom. I'm behind you all the way."

As I took the stage a short time later, I did so with confidence. My son believed in me. He may not remember the misspelled word that ended his last spelling bee, but who cares? The words on that scrap of paper were the ones bound upon our hearts.

DAY 6

"Why do you go to Chapel, How?" he asked me, still going on with his work.

"Because," I said, and then I stopped. Why, indeed?

"Yes," he said, and smiling. "Because you want to? Because you like coming? Because your mother and father come? Because your friends are there? Because it is proper to do on a Sunday? Because there is nothing else to do? Because you like the singing? To hear me preach? Or because you would fear a visitation of fire during the week if you stayed away? Are you brought by fear or by love?"

—Mr. Gryffydd, the rector,
How Green Was My Valley, 365

DAY 7

Breath Prayer: Close your eyes; take several slow, deep breaths; then silently pray this breath prayer in rhythm with your breathing. Repeat several times.

Your word is a lamp . . .
and your teaching a light.

— Light your Sabbath Celebration candle. Sit quietly for five minutes.
— Read the Bible passage for this week: Proverbs 6:20–22.
— Quietly reflect on sources of light—sun, moon, lamp, candle, and so on—and visualize them one by one. Notice the varying amounts of light each provides.
— Read several of the following Bible passages that refer to light: Genesis 1:3; Psalm 4:6; Psalm 27:1; Psalm 119:105; Isaiah 2:5; Isaiah 42:6; Isaiah 60:1; Matthew 5:14–15; John 1:5; Acts 13:47; Acts 26:13; Romans 13:12; 2 Corinthians 6:14; James 1:17; 1 Peter 2:9; 1 John 1:5; Revelation 22:5.
— In your journal, jot down the Bible passages that captivate you. Or write about a source of light that has special meaning to you (for example, your grandmother's lamp that you now use when you read).

— Thank God for all the sources of inner and outer light.

Six days a week are set apart for your daily duties and regular work, but the seventh day is a day of rest dedicated to the Lord your God. (Deut. 5:12)

WEEK 2

DAY 1

Read the following Bible passage each day this week: Matthew 4:1–11.

> Then Jesus was led up by the Spirit into the wilderness to be tempted by the devil. He fasted forty days and forty nights, and afterwards he was famished. The tempter came and said to him, "If you are the Son of God, command these stones to become loaves of bread." But he answered, "It is written,
>
> > 'One does not live by bread alone,
> > > but by every word that comes from the mouth of God.'"
>
> Then the devil took him to the holy city and placed him on the pinnacle of the temple, saying to him, "If you are the Son of God, throw yourself down; for it is written,
>
> > 'He will command his angels concerning you,'
> > > and 'On their hands they will bear you up,
> > so that you will not dash your foot against a stone.'"
>
> Jesus said to him, "Again it is written, 'Do not put the Lord your God to the test.'"

Again, the devil took him to a very high mountain and showed him all the kingdoms of the world and their splendor; and he said to him, "All these I will give you, if you will fall down and worship me." Jesus said to him, "Away with you, Satan! for it is written,

> 'Worship the Lord your God,
> and serve only him.'"

Then the devil left him, and suddenly angels came and waited on him.

Spirit Booster: Reaching In
Is there a particular temptation with which you struggle on an ongoing basis? Write it on a piece of paper and then shred or burn it. Hand over the temptation to Christ with the prayer,

> "Jesus, you know what it is to be tempted. Take this temptation away from me, so that I may worship and serve God. Amen."

Spirit Booster: Reaching Out
The thought of having angels waiting on you is a lovely thought! Do your best to be an "angel" to someone else who needs some extra tender-loving care.

DAY 2
Learning to Say "No"

Temptation comes in many forms, but not always in the way we expect.

The Scripture passage about Jesus being tempted by the devil leads us to believe that temptations come in the guise of evil. Often, however, temptations come dressed in beautiful garments and speaking in sweet voices that make it hard for us to resist.

I get a lot of requests to teach and speak to groups. Can you come to the school and talk to the kids about writing? Will you come to my writers' group and give us some advice about getting published? Would you teach this class, speak at this conference, read this manuscript, write this Bible study, serve on this church committee?

How can I say no? These are all great offers. Every one of them has value, and I am tempted to say yes to them all.

I struggle with a chronic illness that leaves me in pain and with a low supply of energy. There have been several times when I've had to take a leave of absence from my pastoral duties in order to regain a measure of health. During one such episode, a friend told me that I had to learn to say no. She said that when she was offered wonderful opportunities, all of which she found enticing but which she knew would be more than she could juggle if she accepted them all, she asked herself this question: "What is it that only I can do?" It sounded so simple, but I decided to try to put it into action as I started back to my regular routine.

What is it that only I can do?

I am the only one who can be a wife to my husband. I am the only one who can be a mother to my children. I am the only one who can write the books I've agreed to write. I am the only one who can be "me" to my friends.

Sure, I can do lots of other things, and I want to say yes when offers come my way. But when the good offers begin to weigh upon my shoulders and get in the way of my being a wife, mother, pastor, writer, and friend, I ask myself again, "What is it that only I can do?" I turn the question into a prayer: "God, what is it that you need me to do? And what can I *not* do that someone else can?"

I find that by turning the question into a prayer, I allow

God to help me put aside the pride that sometimes makes me think, "I am the *only one* who can do that." I let God guide me into making better decisions about my life. And I seek God's blessing in saying yes and in saying no.

God hasn't let me down yet.

DAY 3
Desert Traveler

Desert traveler.

Before you stretches nothingness,
    barren, endless, vast,
    not even a horizon
    on which to set your course.

Here, in the desert,
    fists of fire beat upon you
    and darkness settles
    like a shroud.

Here, in the desert,
    you must leave behind the load of rocks
    you drag with you through life.
    Cast aside the stones of shame, regret, control.
Their weight will kill you here, in the desert.

But carry only the cup of new life,
    and sip from its cooling waters.
    Or pour it out upon your head
    and be baptized in the dust.
For from dust we have come,
    and to dust we shall return.

Remember,
> It was the Spirit who led Jesus to this place.
> So take off your shoes,
> and step upon the scorching soil,
> then bow down and kiss the earth.
>> For the ground on which you walk is holy.

DAY 4

Lord Jesus, you were tempted; help us when we are tempted.

When we are tempted, help us,
Always to remember those who love us and trust us and
    believe in us, and whose hearts would be broken if we
    brought disgrace upon ourselves;
Never to do anything which would bring us regret,
    remorse, and shame to follow it;
Never to do anything which we would have to hide, and
    about which we should be ashamed that others should
    know;
Never to do anything which would injure anyone else;
Always to remember that whatever we say or do you
    hear and see it.

Save us from ever being carried away by the heat or the
    impulse or the passion of the moment, and so
    forgetting the consequences of the thing we do.

Help us never to disobey our conscience and never to do
    anything which would take away our own self-respect.

Help us to make
  Our pleasure such that we would never wish to hide it;
  Our work such that we never need to be ashamed of it;
  Our conduct to others such that we will never regret it.

At all times keep
  Our thoughts pure and our words true;
  Our actions honourable and our bodies clean.

Help us so to live that we can take everything in life and
  show it to you.

Amen.

—William Barclay, *A Barclay Prayer Book*, 270–71

CO CO

DAY 5
Taking the Easy Way Out

I've never been to a rock concert where this has happened, but I've seen it in movies: one of the musicians on stage decides to leap out into the audience, trusting that he or she will be caught by the outstretched arms and hands of the fans and then carried to safety on a wave of enthusiastic cheers.

I think of this scene when I read Matthew's account of the temptation of Jesus. In the second temptation, the devil challenges Jesus to throw himself from the highest peak of the temple and to use the angels like a trampoline to bounce back to safety.

Jesus is not just being tempted to hurl himself into the arms of the angels. He is being tempted to use his divine status to avoid the suffering and death that waits for him down the road he is destined to travel.

The temptation to take the easy way out of a tough situation is one that none of us escapes. Need to lose weight? Take this pill and you can drop pounds without ever lifting a finger! Your best friend hurt your feelings? Just act like nothing happened and bury your hurt deep down inside where nobody—especially your friend—will ever see it. Feeling spiritually empty? Blame God! Why shoulder the responsibility when you can shrug it off onto larger shoulders?

Taking the easy way out might seem the thing to do at the time, but it can leave you feeling even more empty as time goes on.

Beauty that is only skin deep is still beauty. Faith that is only skin deep isn't faith at all.

We don't necessarily have to look forward to wrestling with the challenges of faith and life. But we can look backwards afterwards and be glad that we did.

No diet pill in the world can do the work of exercise. There's something rewarding about stretching those muscles and then seeing the results. A true friend would want you to say when she has hurt your feelings, so that the wound can heal and not be covered and left to fester. The Christian who takes faith to the next level will find that God isn't going to leave when the going gets tough.

At the beginning of Matthew's account of Jesus' temptation, we are told that the Spirit led Jesus into the wilderness to be tempted. At the end, the angels came and waited on him. Even in the wilderness, tempted by the devil, Jesus was surrounded by the unfailing support and love of God.

It's nice to know that at the beginning and end of whatever challenges we face, we are framed between the Holy Spirit and the angels.

DAY 6

"It is not in the still calm of life . . . that great characters are formed. . . . Great necessities call out great virtues."
—Abigail Adams, *Scholastic Treasury of Quotations for Children,* 42

DAY 7

Breath Prayer: Close your eyes; take several slow, deep breaths; then silently pray this breath prayer in rhythm with your breathing. Repeat several times.

You alone, O God . . .
do I worship and serve.

— Light your Sabbath Celebration candle. Sit quietly for five minutes.
— Read the Bible passage for this week: Matthew 4:1–11.
— Quietly reflect on Jesus' responses to temptation, remembering that he had been in the wilderness without food for forty days.
— Jesus was tempted with food, protection, and power. Which of these temptations are most difficult for you to resist? Be as specific as you can.
— In your journal, write the answers to the previous question.
— Use the verse from the Lord's Prayer, "Lead me not into temptation," naming specific temptations.

What we are *depends on what* the Sabbath is *to us.*
(Abraham Joshua Heschel, 89)

WEEK 3

DAY 1

Read the following Bible passage each day this week: Psalm 91:14–16 (it follows the quote used by Jesus about the angels guarding us).

> Those who love me, I will deliver;
> I will protect those who know my name.
> When they call to me, I will answer them;
> I will be with them in trouble,
> I will rescue them and honor them.
> With long life I will satisfy them,
> and show them my salvation.

Spirit Booster: Reaching In
Thinking back over your life, who or what made you feel protected? Can you relate any of these to images of God? (For example: I always felt protected in my mother's arms. God protects me like my mother's arms.)

Spirit Booster: Reaching Out
Is there a shelter for abused women in your area? Find out more about it and pray for those who seek protection there, or who are in abusive relationships but don't know how to find safety.

DAY 2
Throwing Words Around

At my evening Bible Study one night, a woman shared a story about the Bible drills she experienced in her church as a young girl. All the students had to hold their Bibles above their heads as the teacher shouted out a Bible verse. The students repeated the verse, then rushed to see who could find the passage the fastest. The more familiar the students were with the Bible, the quicker they were inclined to find the verse—and to win the reward, the prize which was that week's big incentive.

I think our churches need to do more to motivate youth and adults to learn the Bible. Memorizing Scripture passages is a good idea. Yet memorizing is one thing, and understanding is another.

The psalm for this week is the one quoted in Matthew 4. The curious part about this is that it isn't Jesus who quotes the psalm; it is the devil. Which just goes to show that anyone can quote a verse out of context to serve a particular purpose.

Knowing the words and living them are two different things. The devil is good at throwing words around. Jesus refuses to throw words around—literally—for Jesus, the Word, refuses to throw himself down, as the devil tempts him to do. Jesus refuses to do anything that abuses the power that has been entrusted to him.

Learning the words is indeed a worthy endeavor. Learning and living the Word is the best reward of all.

DAY 3

God of power,
God of people,
You are the life of all
that lives,
energy
that fills the earth,
vitality
that brings to birth,
the impetus
toward making whole
whatever is bruised
or broken.
In You we grow
to know the truth
that sets all creation free.
You are the song
the whole earth sings,
the promise
liberation brings,
now and forever.

—Miriam Therese Winter,
WomanPrayer, WomanSong, 109

DAY 4

"O Lord, the house of my soul is narrow; enlarge it that you may enter it. It is ruined. O repair it! It displeases your sight; I confess it. I know. But who shall cleanse it, or to whom shall I cry but unto you? Cleanse me from my secret faults, O Lord, and spare your servant from strange sins."

—Augustine, *The One Year Book of Personal Prayer,*
April 3

DAY 5
What's in a Name?

One of the biggest challenges in a growing church is remembering people's names. When a new person visits the church, and then someone remembers and calls that person by name the next time he or she visits, it means a lot. I try very hard to learn a person's name. When I get it right, I get a lot of credit. When I get it wrong, it bothers me tremendously. Everyone wants to be called by name, because a name is more than just a name—it is a big part of our identity.

Names carry a lot of weight and purpose in the Bible. We lose a lot of that in the translation. In the Hebrew, there are many names for God, but in our English translations, many of the names are condensed into the one most familiar to us: God. Names of people indicate significant life transitions, such as when Jacob is renamed "Israel" after his wrestling match on the banks of the Jabbok river. Simon is given the name "Peter," or "rock," when Jesus designates the disciple as the one upon whom he will build the church (Matt. 16:18).

Knowing someone's name indicates the beginning of— or the extension of—a relationship with another person. You cannot be a close friend with someone if you don't even know that person's name!

Given the importance of names in the Bible and in our own lives, it is no surprise that God wants to be known by name, too. "I will protect those who know my name," God says in Psalm 91. God wants us to have enough of a relationship that we can call God by name. Starting a prayer with "Hey, you" just doesn't cut it.

The Amplified Bible expands upon the words "my name" in Psalm 91 to include "has a personal knowledge of My mercy, love, and kindness—trusts and relies on Me." This expanded understanding clearly shows that there's more to calling God by name than just calling God by name.

Establishing and nurturing a relationship with God takes time, energy, effort, and a willingness to work at it, as with any significant relationship. In a time of trouble or need, when we call upon God's name, God hears us. We are much more likely to reach out to God, to call God by name, to ask for help, when we feel close enough to God that we are not afraid to do so.

"When you call to me, I will answer you," says God.

What's in a name? Everything, if that name is God's.

DAY 6

"I have to try, but I do not have to succeed. Following Christ has nothing to do with success as the world sees it. It has to do with love."

—Madeleine L'Engle, *Walking on Water*, 151

DAY 7

Breath Prayer: Close your eyes; take several slow, deep breaths; then silently pray this breath prayer in rhythm with your breathing. Repeat several times.

When I call to you,
you answer me.

— Light your Sabbath Celebration candle. Sit quietly for five minutes.
— Read the Bible passage for this week: Psalm 91:14–16.
— Quietly reflect on God's promise to protect you, to answer you, to rescue you, and to honor you.
— How amazing it is that God honors *you!* In what ways do you honor God?
— In your journal, write down those times when God has rescued you or has been with you in a time of trouble.
— Pray, using the words of Psalm 91:14–16, and allow a time of silence to listen to God's answers to you.

Let the words of my mouth and the meditation of my heart
be acceptable to you, O Lord, my rock and my redeemer.
(Ps. 19:14)

WEEK 4

DAY 1

Read the following Bible passage each day this week: James 1:12–13.

> Blessed is anyone who endures temptation. Such a one has stood the test and will receive the crown of life that the Lord has promised to those who love him. No one, when tempted, should say, "I am being tempted by God"; for God cannot be tempted by evil and he himself tempts no one.

Spirit Booster: Reaching In
In your journal, jot down a temptation that you have resisted or overcome, and give yourself a pat on the back along with giving thanks to God.

Spirit Booster: Reaching Out
Pray for someone you know who is struggling with temptation.

DAY 2
Gathering Rocks and Stacking Blocks

I've lost count of the number of times I've heard someone tell me, "The Lord doesn't give you any more than you can handle." Usually, this wisdom is offered when the weight of the world seems to be pressing down upon a person's shoulders. The implication is that God is the one piling rocks in our daily backpacks, stopping just short of cramming in the final pebble that replicates the straw that pushed that poor camel over the edge.

This kind of theology reminds me of one of my favorite childhood games, Blockhead. The rules were simple: players alternated stacking small, oddly shaped pieces of colored wood, one on top of the other, until one added the piece that caused the whole tower to come toppling down.

I believe that God gives us strength and courage to handle what life dishes out. I do not believe that God keeps stacking problems upon us like those little blocks of wood, to see how much we can handle before our psyches come tumbling down.

In the book of James we read that "blessed are those who endure temptation" but that "God cannot be tempted by evil and he himself tempts no one" (1:13). God isn't gathering rocks or stacking blocks upon us, waiting to see us fall. In Christ, God offers to take that backpack, rocks and all, and to carry that pack for us. In Christ, God puts out a hand to stop the placement of that final block that will cause us to topple over.

The Lord doesn't give you any more than you can handle, that's true. It's not because God knows when to stop loading you down. It's because God is in the business of taking our burdens, not giving them in the first place.

DAY 3
the space between

this was all a dream,
i think.

what did the world look like
(its contours and colors)
before the cyclones came,
before storms kicked up ordinary time
and twisted it,
spindled it,
into oblivion?

all i remember is,
the trains roared out of the station,
slaves to some awful schedule, and
the house trembled and went black —

no time to find a closet,
no time to open windows
(are you supposed to open windows?
notimetolookitup)
just time to collapse to the floor,
put my body over yours,
and for once
you don't giggle from my grip
for once
you just grab on and lie still
in this chaos between kansas and oz.

outside the picture window
here's the picture:

a snaking column of storm
taunts
poises
strikes;
glass shatters,
i grip harder,
hold on
hold on
and i do, but it's
time
that gets sucked away,

day splinters into night,

night whirls into morning

is it morning?
it is still.

eventually
i pry myself off the floor
and stand:
and the debris is terrible

but i have survived
and so have you;
so the wreckage is bathed
in technicolor hope.

a work in progress
   —MaryAnn McKibben Dana
     (unpublished)

DAY 4

Give me, O Lord, a steadfast heart, which no unworthy
    affection may drag downwards;
give me an unconquered heart, which no tribulation can
    wear out;
give me an upright heart, which no unworthy purpose
    may tempt aside.
Bestow on me also, O Lord my God, understanding to
    know you,
diligence to seek you,
wisdom to find you,
and a faithfulness that may finally embrace you,
through Jesus Christ our Lord. Amen.

              —Thomas Aquinas, *The One Year Book*
                of Personal Prayer, January 5

DAY 5
Everyone Wins!

The pageant is down to the final five contestants. Forty-five
women have been eliminated one by one, after parading
around in swimsuits and ball gowns; dancing, singing, and
playing piano; answering questions and proclaiming their
desire for world peace. The tension mounts as the fifth run-
ner-up is named and whisked offstage, followed quickly by
the fourth-, third-, and second-place winners (who are feeling more like losers at this point). Finally, the winner is
announced, the sparkly crown is pinned to her hair, which is
stiff as a wet flag frozen in sub-zero weather, and the band
strikes up the oft-sung solo "Here she comes, Miss America."

    The dreams and efforts of forty-nine women are dashed

to bits in a moment, because there is only one crown to win, one woman who will wear it.

I'm not a big fan of beauty pageants, but that doesn't mean I don't watch them from time to time. Yet the whole concept of one person being deemed more worthy than all the rest doesn't sit well with me. It's not just beauty pageants that operate in this way. Sports are just as focused on one winner and multiple losers. Politics, the same. In truth, it's hard to name exceptions to the rule that "the best man (or woman) wins."

Thank goodness, God's intention for humankind isn't patterned after a beauty pageant, sports event, or political race. We who love God are all winners! We don't have to compete against each other. We just have to believe in the love of God and the forgiveness we are offered in Jesus Christ. There can be more than one winner in the quest for new life.

A team of mentally challenged youngsters played a game of ice hockey. The puck got knocked around all over the ice, but nobody scored. When the referee's whistle blew to mark the end of the scoreless game, the goalie on one of the teams threw her hands up with glee. "Everybody won!" she exclaimed. "Everybody won!"

There is an unending supply of crowns to hand out to those who love God, who face the temptations and troubles of life with steadfast faith and trust in the One in whom all things are possible. Everybody wins!

If only the rest of the world worked that way.

DAY 6

"Nothing great was ever done without much enduring."
—St. Catherine of Siena, *The Westminster Collection of Christian Quotations*, 89

DAY 7

Breath Prayer: Close your eyes; take several slow, deep breaths; then silently pray this breath prayer in rhythm with your breathing. Repeat several times.

Christ, you promise me
the crown of life.

— Light your Sabbath Celebration candle. Sit quietly for five minutes.
— Read the Bible passage for this week: James 1:12–13.
— Quietly reflect on the times when you have blamed God for your problems, remembering the promise in Scripture that God never tempts anyone.
— Have you placed temptation in the path of another person, either intentionally or not? One example would be the tendency to speak badly of other people and to invite others to do the same. Ask God to help you resist the urge to lead others into temptation.
— In your journal, write down temptations that you face regularly (for example, I drink way too much soda pop) and then temptations that are of a spiritual nature (I am tempted to avoid going to church when I've had a busy week).
— Ask a blessing upon you and those you know who have resisted or overcome temptation.

"The Sabbath was made for humankind; and not
humankind for the Sabbath." (Mark 2:27)

APRIL
RENEWAL

WEEK 1

DAY 1

Read the following Bible passage each day this week: Isaiah 40:28–31.

Have you not known? Have you not heard?
The LORD is the everlasting God,
    the Creator of the ends of the earth.
He does not faint or grow weary;
    his understanding is unsearchable.
He gives power to the faint,
    and strengthens the powerless.
Even youths will faint and be weary,
    and the young will fall exhausted;
but those who wait for the Lord shall renew their strength,
    they shall mount up with wings like eagles,
they shall run and not be weary,
    they shall walk and not faint.

Spirit Booster: Reaching In
Take ten extra minutes each day this week (or every day, if you wish!) to sit in solitude and be renewed by the presence of God.

Waiting can be agonizing, especially if someone is sitting at a doctor's office or at a medical facility waiting for a test or test results. Offer to sit and wait with a friend. The time for them will go much more quickly, and your presence can be a reminder of the presence of God.

DAY 2
Wingspan

The bald eagle was my favorite bird when I was growing up. Perhaps my love for the majestic, white-capped flyer foreshadowed my own premature, white hair. If a white-headed bird is considered elegant, then maybe people should take a clue from nature.

The wingspan of a female bald eagle extends from 70 to 90 inches from wingtip to wingtip. Ninety inches—about eight and a half feet—that's quite a stretch! A seven-foot-tall pro basketball player seems enormously tall, but the eagle is over a foot longer if measured by its wingspan.

The wings of an eagle are long and broad, which make them perfect for soaring. The feathers at the tips of the wings are tapered so that when the wings are fully extended, the tips are spread far apart. This helps reduce turbulence as air passes over the wings. When an eagle is soaring, there is no "fasten your seat belt" light flashing overhead!

Eagles make great use of thermals, currents of warm air that rise from the landscape below. The thermals and updrafts aid the eagles as they soar so that they can preserve energy by rarely needing to flap their wings. When eagles make their long-distance migrations, they ride high in a thermal, then glide downward to catch the next burst of rising air, which carries them along until the next. They repeat this over and over, making it possible for them to travel long distances without wearing out.

The prophet Isaiah writes that the Lord never grows weary; that the faint are given power, and the powerless are given strength. Those who wait on the Lord—who put their faith and trust in God—are carried along on wings like eagles. Wings that are broad and strong and safe and smooth. Wings that soar and glide and ride the rising currents. Wings that protect and wings that carry us without any effort at all.

Close your eyes. Imagine, in your weariness, being lifted onto those strong, broad wings and sailing, soaring, and gliding into eternity.

No wonder I love eagles so much. They remind me of God.

DAY 3
On Wings of Eagles

You perch on the edge
of my bed, ready
to fly, cradling my fingers
in your palm like a butterfly,
afraid to crush fragile wings.
Swallowed tears wash words
back down your throat, where
both remain, undigested.

Don't look at me like that,
seeing only death.
I'm living now,
you're dying, too,
but you don't know it.
The candle yet burns,

no longer a flame, but still
an ember glowing in the dark.
Do not extinguish me too soon.

And when the ashen wick
is cold and all that's left
a form of wax,
remember me, and weep not.
For I breathe free and soar
on wings of eagles.
(For Clem, March 1993)

DAY 4

O God, you are our refuge.
  When we are exhausted by life's efforts;
  When we are bewildered by life's problems;
  When we are wounded by life's sorrows:
    We come for refuge to you.

O God, you are our strength.
  When our tasks are beyond our powers;
  When our temptations are too strong for us;
  When duty calls for more than we have to give to it:
    We come for strength to you.

O God, it is from you that all goodness comes.
  It is from you that our ideals come;
  It is from you that there comes to us
    the spur of high desire and the restraint of conscience.
  It is from you that there has come the strength
    to resist any temptation,
    and to do any good thing.

And now as we pray to you,
   Help us to believe in your love,
      so that we may be certain
      that you will hear our prayer;
   Help us to believe in your power,
      so that we may be certain
      that you are able to do for us
      above all that we ask or think;
   Help us to believe in your wisdom,
      so that we may be certain
      that you will answer,
      not as our ignorance asks,
      but as your perfect wisdom knows best.

All this we ask through Jesus Christ our Lord. Amen.
   —William Barclay, *A Barclay Prayer Book,* 134–35

DAY 5
Running the Race

One year, my husband decided to start running marathons. He started training in June and ran the Chicago Marathon that same October. Since the race is always on Sunday morning, I had to stay home and "hold down the fort," or church, while he went off to run the good race.

The family planned to celebrate upon his return home. We held off eating lunch, preparing to fill up at a nice restaurant, a treat we rarely could afford in those days.

At about 2:30 p.m., Greg walked in the door. "Walked" may be putting it too strongly. He crept in the door. He shuffled. He could barely move. He fell into a tub of hot bath water and decided it might be a good place to spend the rest of his life. The kids and I, starving and eager to get out of the house, had little sympathy to offer.

Although he swore he would never run another

marathon again, he did. Four more times. The kids and I learned from the first marathon, however. We ate out before he got home.

I don't know how anyone runs—or runs/walks—or even runs/walks/sits/runs/walks/crawls for twenty-six straight (and winding and up-and-down) miles. I'm lucky to dash out to the mailbox and back before I collapse. If even the youths will faint and be weary and fall down, exhausted, I don't think there's much chance for me.

Isaiah promises that God never faints or grows weary, and that those who wait upon the Lord shall have their own strength renewed. I doubt this means that we will all be running marathons, at least not the kind that takes special shoes. But there are other races to be run.

A young soldier fighting in a war is seriously injured when the vehicle in which he is traveling is shattered by a bomb. He falls to the ground, unconscious from a nearly fatal head wound. At the risk of his own life, one of his comrades, himself shot and bleeding, picks up the young man and carries him to a safe place where he receives the medical attention that saves his life.

In Christ, God risks God's own life in order to carry each of us to safety when we are too worn down to go even one step further on our own.

When life itself seems like a marathon, and our spirits are weary to the core, God picks us up and carries us across the finish line.

DAY 6

"[S]ave yourself from these general themes and seek those which your own everyday life offers you; describe your sorrows and desires, passing thoughts and the belief in some sort of beauty—describe all these with loving, quiet,

humble sincerity, and use, to express yourself, the things in your environment, the images from your dreams, and the objects of your memory."
—Rainer Maria Rilke, *Letters to a Young Poet*, 19

DAY 7

Breath Prayer: Close your eyes; take several slow, deep breaths; then silently pray this breath prayer in rhythm with your breathing. Repeat several times.

Lift me, O Lord,
on wings of eagles.

— Light your Sabbath Celebration candle. Sit quietly for five minutes.
— Read the Bible passage for this week: Isaiah 40:28–31.
— Quietly reflect on the promise that the day will come when we are no longer weary and worn down by this life, but filled with endless energy, soaring on wings.
— Have you ever wished you had wings like a bird? Where would you go and what would you want to see? Imagine how it would feel to float on a breeze high above the earth and to look down on the beauty of creation.
— In your journal, write down what wears you down. What makes you exhausted? What fills your spirit with energy?
— Ask God's blessing upon those who are weary and worn down.

[W]hen we experience being enveloped by Sabbath time, we become people who are not enslaved to time. (Marva Dawn, 123)

WEEK 2

DAY 1

Read the following Bible passage each day this week: Matthew 17:1–8.

> Six days later, Jesus took with him Peter and James and his brother John and led them up a high mountain, by themselves. And he was transfigured before them, and his face shone like the sun, and his clothes became dazzling white. Suddenly there appeared to them Moses and Elijah, talking with him. Then Peter said to Jesus, "Lord, it is good for us to be here; if you wish, I will make three dwellings here, one for you, one for Moses, and one for Elijah." While he was still speaking, suddenly a bright cloud overshadowed them, and from the cloud a voice said, "This is my Son, the Beloved; with him I am well pleased; listen to him!" When the disciples heard this, they fell to the ground and were overcome by fear. But Jesus came and touched them, saying, "Get up and do not be afraid." And when they looked up, they saw no one except Jesus himself alone.

Spirit Booster: Reaching In
What do you fear? Imagine Jesus touching you on the shoulder and saying, "Do not be afraid."

Spirit Booster: Reaching Out
Do you have children? Tell them how beloved they are and how much they please you. This applies even if your children are adults! And if you don't have children, "adopt" one—a neighbor, a child in church, a friend's grandchild—and tell them the same thing.

DAY 2
A Glimpse of Heaven

I used to believe that heaven was that place just beyond the clouds, where the sun broke through and cast shimmering fingers of light, reaching down to earth. Even now, when I see slanting shards of light reaching from the sky to earth, I imagine that heaven is right there, almost within reach. It's a glimpse of heaven, at the very least; a precious peek at the place where the light of God's face shines brighter than any star, where not even the darkest storm clouds can begin to dim it.

When I read the story of the transfiguration of Jesus, I try to picture the brilliance with which Jesus blazed before Peter, James, and John. What shot through the minds of that apostolic trio when Moses and Elijah, two Old Testament characters that had been dead for centuries, appeared there with Jesus? Peter was so terrified he offered to play carpenter and build homes for everyone. Then, right before the disciples' eyes, a thick cloud dropped down around them like a stage curtain, and when it lifted, Moses and Elijah were gone, leaving only Jesus and three stunned men.

This story is simply beyond our understanding. We don't know why God chose that moment to reveal to the disciples the glory of Jesus. We don't know why Moses and Elijah showed up out of nowhere and why they disappeared as fast as they had come. We don't know what happened between God and Jesus when the cloud cut them off from the disciples. All we know is that something miraculous happened. The disciples saw a little glimpse of heaven that day.

Perhaps Jesus and God put their heads together and talked about what was going to happen in the not-so-distant future when Jesus would hang on a cross. Perhaps God simply wrapped his heavenly arms around his only Son and let him know how much he loved Jesus. After all, it does say that a voice from the cloud boomed out, "This is my Son, the Beloved; listen to him!" I imagine the sound of that voice, bursting with pride and also with agony at knowing what even Jesus' most loyal followers were about to do to him.

But even that is a glimpse of heaven. Jesus and God, together as one. God knowing what his own creation would do to his Son, and loving them still. Jesus, reflecting the glory of God like a mirror catching a sunbeam, sending it skittering in all directions. A love so great that the disciples were left speechless, carrying the story of that day to their own crosses and graves.

I think that is all we can ask for on this earth: glimpses of heaven. To try and understand the glory of heaven in its full magnitude would be impossible. We'd split like a tree struck with lightning. It's more than our mortal minds can handle. Yet we are blessed every day with glimpses of heaven. If we look for them, if we are aware, we'll see them as clearly as the sun sifting through the clouds after a storm.

DAY 3
God Is the One

God is the One
  who awakens and lifts
    my body from sleep,
    my eyes from earth to sky,
    my heart from silence to joy.
The One who awakens
  my spirit
    from death to life.
The One who is risen
  raises me.

DAY 4
In Your Light

God of transformation,
In your light
  we are forced to see you as you are
in all your glory
  and splendor
and it is frightening
because we can no longer pretend
that you are who we think you are.
You Are Who You Are.
Dazzling as the sun, you are
  the Son,
    The Beloved.
And we do not know what that means.
  Yet we do.

God of transfiguration,
In your light
  we are forced to see ourselves as we are
  in all our gory—
    offenders,
  and it is frightening
  because we can no longer pretend
  that we are who we think we are.
  We Are Not Who We Want to Be.
  Shadowed by the Son, we are
    the ones
    who put you in tents
    and boxes
  where we do not have to look at you.
    Yet we do.

In your light
  we try to hide
  but we can hide no longer, for
in your light
  the circles under our eyes deepen
  the circles around our lives tighten
  and we fall to the ground
    in sorrow and in shame.
In your light,
  we are blinded
  too bright to see,
    too bright not to.
And so we fall down
  and tremble
    and then you touch our shoulder
  and say,
  donotbeafraid.

Get up.

Amen.

DAY 5
Too Close to See

It came as a shocking realization. I didn't know my own children.

Okay, so maybe that statement is a bit extreme. But I clearly remember watching my teenagers interact with their friends one day and realizing that there was so much I didn't know about these people I thought I knew so well. Up until then, I felt as though I were the one who knew them best: I had carried them in my womb, given birth to them, spent days and nights without end caring for them, and watched them grow—much too quickly. Watching them with their friends, however, it struck me that as much as I did know about them—their favorite foods, the age each one was when he or she began to walk, their different skills and gifts, what made them tick (and what ticked them off)—there was that much, and more, I didn't know.

When we live with people, or see them on a daily basis, it's a challenge to see them clearly, as *they* are, not just what we assume to be true.

I can let the disciples off the hook when I think of their inability to see Jesus clearly. They saw him perform miracles: feed thousands of people, heal the blind, stand up to the authorities. They also ate with him, traveled with him, saw him when he was tired and withdrawn, and probably when he had a case of bed-head or morning breath. They knew he was the Son of God, and yet they didn't. It's hard enough for us to understand the combination of divine and human in Jesus. Imagine those who spent every day with him trying to figure it out.

Jesus takes Peter, James, and John up to the mountaintop, and while they are there, Jesus dissolves into a brilliant light. Before they know it, Moses and Elijah join the party, and the disciples don't even seem fazed by two dead men appearing out of nowhere. What will it take for them to really see Jesus? What will it take to shake them from their acceptance back into an attitude of awe?

It takes one voice, falling like raindrops from a passing cloud: "This is my Son, the Beloved; with him I am well pleased;" and then a clap of thunder: "listen to him!" They've heard this voice before. They've heard these words before. But where? And when?

In the far recesses of their minds, they remember. They remember Jesus climbing out of the Jordan river, dripping wet, and the heavens splitting open like an overripe gourd. The voice. The words: "This is my Son, the Beloved, with whom I am well pleased" (Matt. 3:17). Jesus' baptism—when Jesus was first revealed to them as the Son of God. The disciples drop to the ground, trembling, perhaps expecting the end of the world.

When they feel Jesus' fingertips on their shoulders and hear his gentle words, "Get up," they glance around through the squints in their eyes. What will they see? Who will they find, standing there with Jesus? God, perhaps?

But nobody is there, except for the three disciples. And Jesus.

They're still shaking as they look at him. It's as if they are seeing Jesus for the very first time.

⟜⟞⟝⟞

DAY 6

"I love the recklessness of faith. First you leap, and then you grow wings."

—William Sloane Coffin, *Credo*, 7

DAY 7

Breath Prayer: Close your eyes; take several slow, deep breaths; then silently pray this breath prayer in rhythm with your breathing. Repeat several times.

With Christ,
I am well pleased.

— Light your Sabbath Celebration candle. Sit quietly for five minutes.
— Read the Bible passage for this week: Matthew 17:1–8.
— Quietly reflect on how the disciples became afraid when the glory of Christ was revealed to them, and how Jesus reached out and told them, "Do not be afraid." What tone of voice do you think he used?
— How are your perceptions of Christ shaken by circumstances and events that challenge you?
— In your journal, jot down words that you use to describe Jesus.
— Pray that Christ may be more fully revealed to you.

All our life should be a pilgrimage to the seventh day.
(Abraham Joshua Heschel, 89)

WEEK 3

DAY 1

Read the following Bible passage each day this week:
Psalm 34:4–8.

> I sought the LORD, and he answered me,
>   and delivered me from all my fears.
> Look to him, and be radiant;
>   so your faces shall never be ashamed.
> This poor soul cried, and was heard by the LORD,
>   and was saved from every trouble.
> The angel of the LORD encamps
>   around those who fear him, and delivers them.
> O taste and see that the LORD is good;
>   happy are those who take refuge in him.

Spirit Booster: Reaching In
Take a moment to appreciate each of your five senses:
taste, touch, sight, smell, and hearing. If you have difficulties with any of these (for instance, if your hearing is
impaired), you will be even more aware of what gifts our
senses are.

Spirit Booster: Reaching Out
When you're out and about, look people in the eye, smile,

and say "hello"! That may be just enough to brighten a stranger's day.

DAY 2
A Ring of Angels

In January of 2003, my father found himself in a hospital in Nevada where he lives, facing open heart surgery. I flew west from my home near Chicago and arrived an hour before he was taken to surgery.

The surgery went well, and it seemed that Dad was on the road to a fairly quick recovery. Then everything started going wrong. He developed infections. He couldn't eat. He began to run a fever. He had trouble breathing.

On a Tuesday morning one week after surgery, I sat by his hospital bed and watched him go downhill at a rapid pace. His oxygen levels dropped dangerously low, even while he was being given full oxygen. Within a very short time, doctors and nurses swarmed around his bed, and he was placed back on the respirator and whisked off to Intensive Care. I followed, in a daze at the swiftness with which his situation had so drastically changed.

For the next fourteen hours I sat by his bedside in ICU, watching his heart rate rise and his blood pressure and oxygen levels fall by the minute. The doctors could not figure out what had gone wrong. The staff worked desperately to get him stabilized. What could I do? Nothing! Nothing but sit there and watch my father suffer, knowing that he might not make it through the night.

I sat and held Dad's hand and prayed for him and felt isolated, helpless, and afraid. Yet along with those inevitable feelings, I knew that we were not alone, and not just because of the constant stream of nurses and doctors checking on my father. We were surrounded by prayers and by the presence of the living God, the Christ who suffers with us and walks with us through the valley of shadows.

We are fortunate. My father made it through that dark night, and many more to follow, until he finally returned home sixty-seven days later.

My father doesn't remember that traumatic night. In fact, he doesn't remember the first week of his time in Intensive Care, and that is a mercy. But I remember. I remember every minute.

I think if I had looked hard enough as I sat by my father's side, I might have seen a surprising sight. For I am certain that, there in that hospital room, among the tubes and wires and pumps and needles and gauze, a ring of angels were camped around us.

DAY 3
I See Your Pain

I see your pain
    and want to banish it
        with the wave of a star,
but have no star.

I see your tears
    and want to dry them
        with the hem of an angel's gown,
but have no angel.

I see your heart fallen to the ground
    and want to return it
        wrapped in cloths woven of rainbow,
but have no rainbow.

God is the One
  who has stars, and angels and rainbows,
and I am the one
  God sends to sit beside you
    until the stars come out
      and the angels dry your tears
        and your heart is back in place,
          rainbow blessed.
— Ann Weems, *Searching for Shalom*, 23

DAY 4

O God, our Father, you alone can enable us to accept
  and to obey your commandments and to do your will.

Increase our faith.
  Help us,
    To trust you when the skies are dark;
    To accept that which we cannot understand;
    To be quite sure that all things can work together
      for good for those who love you.

Increase our hope.
  Give us
    The hope which has seen things at their worst,
      and which refuses to despair;
    The hope that is able to fail,
      and yet to try again;
    The hope which can accept disappointment,
      and yet not abandon hope.

Increase our love.
  Help us,
    To love our fellow men and women, as you love
      them;

To love you as you have first loved us;
To love loyalty to our Lord above all other things.

Help us so to love you that your commandments will
never be a weariness and a burden to us, but that it will
be a joy for us to obey them, so that in obedience to you
we may find our perfect freedom, and in doing your will
our peace.

So grant to us,
   To fight the good fight;
   To run the straight race;
   To keep the faith,
      that we may win the glory and the crown.

Hear these our prayers for your love's sake. Amen.
     —William Barclay, *A Barclay Prayer Book,* 116–17

DAY 5
Common Sense

Much is made these days of the multisensory approach to
learning, which states that different people learn in different ways, using different senses. Some people are auditory
learners, able to listen and comprehend the spoken word.
These people do well in classes taught using lectures.
Some are visual learners, needing to see what is being
taught. These people do well with diagrams and the like.
Some folks need touch: give them a problem they can put
their hands on, such as a computer that needs to be fixed,
and they thrive. It's a good thing the world is made up of
various kinds of learners, or else each of us would have to
be a jack-of-all-trades. It's like the image of the body that
the apostle Paul used to describe the church: it takes all

the parts to make a whole. One part is not more important than another.

It strikes me as I read Psalm 34 that in four short verses (4–8), all of the five senses are taken into account:

"I sought the Lord, and he *answered* me . . ." (hear that, all ye auditory learners!).

"Look to him . . ." (visual learners, take note).

"This poor soul *cried*, and was *heard* by the Lord, and was *saved from* every sort of trouble . . ." (verbal, auditory, and some hands-on action by God).

"O *taste* and *see* that the Lord is good . . ." (taste, sight, and smell—since we have to smell something in order to taste it).

So what's my point? I'm not exactly sure. It seems to me, however, that in a "sense" the psalm affirms that God reaches out to us in many different ways. There isn't any one way to experience God. God is going to use our "common senses," so to speak, to be present to us. Where there's a will, there's a way, because it is God's will to be found by each and every one of us.

You may sense the presence of God in the warm touch of the sun shining on your back; or in the sight of the blue lake sparkling in the morning; or in the smell of fresh, baked bread, hot out of the oven; or in the taste of fresh strawberries picked from the vine; or in the sound of a child's laughter; or even in all of these ways. Who's to say we can't "sense" God's presence (maybe we should spell that "*presense*") every which way there is?

Be aware of the ways you experience God in the everyday.

Using the senses God gave us in the first place—why, that's just common sense!

DAY 6

"By the reading of Scripture I am so renewed that all nature seems renewed around me and with me."
— Thomas Merton, *The Westminster Collection of Christian Quotations*, 315

DAY 7

Breath Prayer: Close your eyes; take several slow, deep breaths; then silently pray this breath prayer in rhythm with your breathing. Repeat several times.

O taste and see
that the Lord is good.

— Light your Sabbath Celebration candle. Sit quietly for five minutes.
— Read the Bible passage for this week: Psalm 34:4–8.
— Quietly reflect on the image of being encircled by angels.
— Remember playing hide and seek as a child? Where are the places from which you hide from God and from which you seek God?
— In your journal, write about where you have sought and found God and where you have sought and not found God. In what places, people, or situations might you look for God, where you have never thought to look before?
— Pray for those seeking God, that they might find what they are looking for.

As we celebrate Sabbath, we "invite a time in which we can taste what we have been given, take delight in what we already have, and see that it is good." (Wayne Muller, 126)

WEEK 4

DAY 1

Read the following Bible passage each day this week: Romans 12:2.

> Do not be conformed to this world, but be transformed by the renewing of your minds, so that you may discern what is the will of God—what is good and acceptable and perfect.

Spirit Booster: Reaching In
Society often makes us feel as though we should all be the same. What unique quality of yours do you appreciate most?

Spirit Booster: Reaching Out
Affirm another person's uniqueness—and celebrate it together!

DAY 2
Perfect Antiques

I love antiques. I've always been the sentimental type, cherishing those objects that have been given to me and that once belonged to someone else. I'm not exactly sure when my obsession with antiques began, but I suspect it can be traced back to our years in Pennsylvania when Greg and I were newlyweds, newly ordained and newly poor. Like many people, we didn't start out with much in the way of possessions. For many years, we didn't even own a dresser, but instead used a huge, seminary-reject bookcase in which we stacked our meager piles of clothes. When our first child was on the way, Greg's family carted the old family crib and baby bureau from Chicago to Pittsburgh. I was captivated by the stories of the other family members who had slept in that crib and was delighted to see the names of two little twin girl cousins scratched into the golden wood on the inside of the bureau door. This was wonderful! Our babies would sleep in the crib their father and grandfather and other assorted great-cousins had slept in. When it came to old furniture, I was hooked.

I began scouting around old shops filled with used furniture, and as we added babies to our household, I also added tables, bookcases, and chairs. Perhaps after all those years using that old bookcase to house our clothes, I developed a particular fondness for beautiful, old, affordable dressers. Some people take in stray cats. I take in unwanted dressers.

Antiques get more valuable with age. A scratch here, a ding or dent there, usually adds to the value of the piece. If only we felt that way about people, with signs of aging considered signs of honor. But oh, no! A wrinkle here, a gray hair there, and in the eyes of society our value declines. Get out the face cream. Stock up on hair coloring. For heaven's sake, don't show your age!

Don't let the standards of a youth-oriented society tell you who you are. The book of Romans puts it this way: "Do not be conformed to this world." Our joy comes not from hiding our imperfections but in discerning, or recognizing, the will of God. God wills for you to know that you are loved not for outward appearances but because you belong to God. You belong to God—for all time.

The next time you panic at another sign of your own aging, think of yourself as a perfect antique. After all, that's the way God looks at you.

DAY 3
On a Theme from Nicolas of Cusa

When soul and body feed, one sees
Their differing physiologies.
Firmness of apple, fluted shape
Of celery, or tight-skinned grape
I grind and mangle when I eat,
Then in dark, salt, internal heat,
Annihilate their natures by
The very act that makes them I.

But when the soul partakes of good
Or truth, which are her savoury food,
By some far subtler chemistry
It is not they that change, but she,
Who feels them enter with the state
Of conquerors her opened gate,
Or, mirror-like, digest their ray
By turning luminous as they.
—C. S. Lewis, *Poems*, 70

DAY 4
The other side of the street

Just when we imagine that we have you figured out
you show up working the other side of the street

in your frightening freedom.
You meet us behind and before
as promise and as threat,
and we are overmatched whenever we sit to deal with
    you.
So we bid you to pay less vigorous attention to us
and we bid you to give us the freedom and courage
that we may withstand you
in ways that are proper to you and to us.
We pray in the name of the utterly humble One
whom you therefore exalted.
Give us wisdom and freedom
that we may sense the ways in which we may best live in
    this world
where the last become first and the first become last.
    Amen.

—Walter Brueggemann, *Awed to Heaven,*
Rooted in Earth, 13

DAY 5
Put Your Mind to It

A couple of years before I became President of the Presbyterian Writers Guild, I entered a contest they sponsored
for the "best phrase or logo." My winning entry was
"Jesus died to take away your sins, not your mind." I have
to admit (and I admitted then) that I could not claim
authorship of this clever quote. I first read it on a scrap of
old newspaper pinned to a corkboard in the office of the
church we served fresh out of seminary. I won a T-shirt for
winning the contest, which, if the original writer of that
quote ever shows up, I will willingly hand over, because I
still think that is one of the best quotes I've ever heard.

It seems as though some people do that, however: give

up thinking for themselves and questioning the world because it is seen as a lack of faith. I don't know where this concept came from, because as far as I can tell by reading the Bible, Jesus used his mind and intelligence and challenged everybody else to use theirs. Look at how he always had a quick comeback when an opponent tried to put him on the spot, or the way he knew every aspect of the law and was an expert on scriptural wisdom. Jesus enjoyed a good riddle and an intellectual debate. None of that diminished his faith in the least.

Nor does it diminish ours. Thinking about our Christian faith—what it means, how we are going to live it day by day amidst the challenges that confront us—all can strengthen our faith in positive ways.

Many of the books I write for children ask questions about faith. I get my material in part from figuring out what questions kids are most likely to ask, and in part from the questions asked by real-life kids. When I was writing my book on questions about heaven, I asked my congregation to tell me the questions their own children asked. I was a bit surprised when the adults started coming to me, asking questions they themselves had about heaven. A lot of the adults asked secretly, afraid of looking foolish in front of others. My response: It's okay to ask questions! We should never stop asking questions. How can we expect to find answers if we never ask the questions?

Faith takes faith. There's a lot of trust involved. But asking questions, thinking about what we believe, engaging in a good discussion—why, that's faith, too.

Remember, Jesus died to take away your sins, not your mind. You can bet your life on that.

DAY 6

"Understanding is the reward of faith. Therefore seek not to understand that you may believe, but believe that you may understand."

—St. Augustine of Hippo, *The Westminster Collection of Christian Quotations*, 387

DAY 7

Breath Prayer: Close your eyes; take several slow, deep breaths; then silently pray this breath prayer in rhythm with your breathing. Repeat several times.

Renew my mind, O Christ;
teach me your will.

— Light your Sabbath Celebration candle. Sit quietly for five minutes.
— Read the Bible passage for this week: Romans 12:2.
— Quietly reflect on the words "good," "acceptable," and "perfect."
— What are the ways in which our society and culture teach us that conformity is something to desire?
— In your journal, write down what you believe God's will to be for you.
— Pray for strength not to conform to what others think you should be, but to have the wisdom to know what it is that God wants for you.

The Sabbath is a day for the sake of life. (Abraham Joshua Heschel, 14)

MAY
HOPE

WEEK 1

DAY 1

Read the following Bible passage each day this week: Jeremiah 31:33–34.

> But this is the covenant that I will make with the house of Israel after those days, says the LORD: I will put my law within them, and I will write it on their hearts; and I will be their God, and they shall be my people. No longer shall they teach one another, or say to each other, "Know the LORD," for they shall all know me, from the least of them to the greatest, says the LORD; for I will forgive their iniquity, and remember their sin no more.

Spirit Booster: Reaching In
Who has been an influential person in your life as far as teaching you about faith? Think about the ways that person taught you.

Spirit Booster: Reaching Out
For some of us, it is difficult to talk about our faith with others. Think of one way you might share part of your faith story with someone you know. You might tell a story, talk about an author who has influenced you, or share a

piece of artwork. As you do this, remember that what you share with another person may help to influence or shape that person's life, too!

☙ ❧

DAY 2
Covenant

My husband and I met in seminary. I was in my second year; he was in his first. Neither of us started seminary with the intention of finding a spouse, let alone marrying another clergy person. I didn't even plan to go into ministry when I left my home in southern California and headed east to Princeton. My goal was to get a degree in Christian Education and teach in a church.

Within my first few months at Princeton, I knew that God had other plans for my life. My original goal expanded to include my call to ordained ministry. I was more surprised than anybody.

Greg and I started out as friends, but just as my goal for graduate education expanded the year before, my life goals changed that second year. Less than a year after we met, Greg and I got engaged at Disneyland—the perfect setting for a southern California girl.

We spent the next ten months planning our wedding. We met with a counselor and wrote our own vows. We worked hard to put together all the pieces, especially since we lived in New Jersey and the wedding was going to be in California.

We wanted our wedding to incorporate our future plans to serve as pastors. How could we weave in the promises we made to one another with the pledge we had made to follow God's call into ministry?

Somewhere along the line during those busy months we decided to use the word "covenant" in the wording of our wedding invitations, as well as in the vows we wrote. So our invitations ended up with us inviting people to a "service of worship celebrating our marriage covenant." Our vows began, "I Greg/Kathy, covenant with you, Kathy/Greg, before God and these witnesses. . . ." Okay, so these sound like the kind of vows written by two theology students, I admit. But hey—that's what we were at the time!

Expressing our marriage as a covenant with God said that we weren't just making our promises to each other, but to the only One who could give us what we needed to keep those promises. We believed (and still do) our marriage to be a "contract" between two people, but also between each of us and God. It hasn't made our married lives any easier than anyone else's. We've had our share of ups and downs. Somehow, knowing that we made that covenant with God helps us in the "downs" and keeps us from being smug during the "ups." We know that God is the essential component in the equation.

In all the weddings we've been invited to over the years, I don't think I've ever seen anyone else use the word "covenant" in their invitations. That's too bad. We hold no claim on the word. And if couples started using the word in their invitations and vows, that would be great. Why not start a trend?

DAY 3
Secret

The truth, or so he came
to tell us, will not be caught
and held within the ordered paragraphs
and pages of a treatise or elaborated dogma,
does not lend itself to concise delineation

or precise and tidily presented definition,
is never to be found locked tight inside
those capsulated catch-word phrases,
slogans, live-or-die-for credos that we love
to force down one another's throats.
Rather it is to be glimpsed across a table,
fireside, subway car, or early morning meadow,
a late lingering fragrance, echo of tears
or laughter, a child's response to
this world's daily mystery, a gift revealed
in every moment we can look and listen
to each other, see, and sing that living truth
that woos us, weds us, weaves us in
and through the holy fabric of our days.
            —J. Barrie Shepherd (unpublished)

DAY 4
Forgive Us

O God, you gave us a garden of Eden
    and we chose to wander in deserts of our own making.
You gave us the Light of the world
    and we chose to do our night-crawling.
Forgive us our squandering
    our wandering
        our lack of commitment.
Forget not your covenant with us, O God, and
    choose us still
        to tell your Good News
            to give all that we have
                that all might be one in your Shalom.
            In Jesus' name we pray. Amen.
                —Ann Weems, *Searching for Shalom*, 62

DAY 5
Writer's Block

A couple of years ago I published a book of biographies on the Newbery Medal authors. The Newbery Medal ranks high on the list of most prestigious awards given in the field of children's literature. With awe and trepidation, I began contacting a number of the medalists, all of whom responded with grace, kindness, and willingness to grant interviews to me, a novice and unknown writer.

I asked the authors which questions they were most often asked by children, and the list was amazingly consistent: "Where do you get your ideas?" "Who is your favorite character?" "What do you do when you get writer's block?" My intention was to answer these questions in my book, thus responding to the questions of the hopeful readers, and also to provide a resource that answered other persistent and sometimes tiresome questions.

The question about writer's block elicited a number of diverse and interesting answers. One author declared that the children's questions about writer's block stemmed from the rote and routine assignments given to children in school, such as "Write about your summer vacation." For a child who has answered that question a hundred times already, or who had a plain and uneventful summer, trying to write an essay about it would be like squeezing juice from a dried-up orange. Such assignments, many of the authors agreed, squelched creative writing in children. Watching my own children struggle with these same questions, I couldn't help but agree.

Another Newbery-winning author said that, for her, writer's block wasn't something to fear, but rather a signal that something had gone awry in her writing. If she encountered writer's block in chapter 7, for instance, that meant that she needed to go back through her entire manuscript and find the place where the writing took a wrong turn. By fixing the problem earlier in the manuscript, the "writer's block" that appeared later on vanished. Problem solved. I thought that was a wonderfully positive way to look at something many people considered a huge issue for a writer.

I love the image in Jeremiah about God "writing" the law on our hearts. Okay, so I'm a writer, and I like images that relate to writing. More than that, I love the idea of God's writing over and over again, on each of our hearts, and never getting writer's cramp or writer's block.

Perhaps if God has any trouble writing on our hearts, it's a signal that there is something amiss in our lives, something that needs to be examined and fixed. It might be a problem that goes way back in our personal history, some "block" that keeps us from accepting or believing the word God wishes to carve upon our spirit.

I also love the idea that God writes on our hearts because writing implies words, and it is the Word, after all, that brings all life, and new life, into our hearts in the first place.

DAY 6

"A Christian people doesn't mean a lot of little goody-goodies. The church has plenty of stamina, and isn't afraid of sin. On the contrary, she can look it in the face calmly and even take it upon herself, assume it at times, as Our Lord did. . . .

Look: I'll define you a Christian people by the opposite. The opposite of a Christian people is a people grown sad and old."

—Georges Bernanos, *Diary of a Country Priest*, 18

DAY 7

Breath Prayer: Close your eyes; take several slow, deep breaths; then silently pray this breath prayer in rhythm with your breathing. Repeat several times.

You are my God,
and I am yours.

— Light your Sabbath Celebration candle. Sit quietly for five minutes.
— Read the Bible passage for this week: Jeremiah 31:33–34.
— Quietly reflect on the knowledge of God that is "written" on your heart. Where does that knowledge come from? How does this Scripture passage reinforce God's love for you?
— Is there a difference between "head knowledge" and "heart knowledge"? How would you define each? Which is more active in your life of faith?
— In your journal, reflect on the people or situations that have strengthened your faith. See if any patterns develop or if your list is varied. Remember how the Scripture indicates that we are all equal in God's sight.
— Give thanks for the people who strengthen your faith, and for the beauty of nature that reflects God's goodness.

The higher goal of spiritual living is not to amass a wealth of information, but to face sacred moments. (Abraham Joshua Heschel, 6)

WEEK 2

DAY 1

Read the following Bible passage each day this week: Luke 1:78–79.

> "By the tender mercy of our God,
>   the dawn from on high will break upon us,
> to give light to those who sit in darkness and in the
>   shadow of death,
>   to guide our feet into the way of peace."

Spirit Booster: Reaching In
Peace begins from within each of us. Close your eyes, breathe slowly, and try to center your spirit in a mode of peacefulness.

Spirit Booster: Reaching Out
Is there a situation of conflict in your home, your neighborhood, or your community? Can you offer a peaceful, calming presence in that situation?

DAY 2
Light Source

"I want you to sit back for a moment, close your eyes, and relax—but not too much. Now, make a mental note of all the images and thoughts that come to your mind when you hear the word 'light.' "

This was the opening exercise one week in my Sunday School class. After taking a few minutes to write down our thoughts and images about light, we shared our lists with the rest of the class. It was fascinating to discover that although we began by listing typical sources of light—sun, moon, stars, flashlights, lamps—within a very short time, our imaginations kicked into gear and our lists broadened to include

> Light as safety—because crimes are less likely to
>   happen in a well-lit area than in a darkened place;
> Light as substance, as the absence of weight—such as,
>   "light as a feather" versus "heavy as lead";
> Light as warmth—as in the heat given off by a
>   crackling campfire on a crisp, autumn night;
> Light as life—because plants and trees and people
>   cannot grow without light.

Thinking about light in these various ways led us to remember stories from our lives that had something to do with light. One woman in the class grew up in Africa, the daughter of missionaries. Because of the lack of adequate power sources, each family was allotted only two hours of electricity out of every twenty-four hours. During those two hours, the family made precious use of the time, cooking and reading and listening to the radio, which was their one link with the outside world.

Another woman remembered sitting around the family table, listening to her stepfather tell wonderful stories about her birth father who had died when she was very young. The father and stepfather had been lifelong friends, growing up together in an orphanage. Hearing the stories her stepfather told gave this woman a feeling of warmth, a warmth that still glows these many years later.

When I was a little girl, I was fascinated by Klieg lights—those great, sweeping beams of light that criss-crossed the night sky announcing the opening of a new store or business. Those arms of light moved as graceful as a dancer, and they seemed to come from a source far away, out of reach, like the pot of gold at the end of a rainbow. I was shocked when I saw my first Klieg light up close: the enormous, swirling light bulbs shooting those immense, dancing beams of light into the darkness.

Whether light means safety, substance, warmth, or vision, all light has to have a source. And the source of all light is Christ.

Those Klieg lights had a purpose: Attention, everyone! There's something here you have to see! You don't want to miss it! No matter how far you have to go to get here, it's worth it! Come and find out for yourself! Come and find the source of the light.

Go back to that written or mental list you made with your images of light. Now, add one more item to your list: your name. Because as Christian people, there should be something within us that shouts, "Attention, everyone! There's something here you have to see! You don't want to miss it! No matter how far you have to go to get here, it's worth it! Come and find out for yourself! Come and find the source of the light. It is Jesus, the light of the world."

DAY 3

Hope is that thing with feathers
that perches in the soul
and sings the tune without the words
and never stops . . . at all.
— Emily Dickinson, *The Complete*
Poems of Emily Dickinson, 254

DAY 4

Your light, O God,
dawns from above,
spilling over me like golden honey,
warm and sweet and life-giving,
drizzling across the shadows with streaks of brightness
until the darkness is dispelled.
Set my spirit upon winged feet,
and send me down the path of peace,
the peace which only comes from you.
By your tender mercy,
help me to discover the truth
that I am loved
by the one who is the light,
Jesus Christ my Savior.
Amen.

DAY 5
Stars in Jars

I remember when I was four years old, playing outside on a warm, California evening as my parents chatted with the neighbors. As day folded into night, I looked up at the cheerful stars. I longed to reach out and touch one, but they were beyond my reach.

I saw a star hurtle toward earth, then vanish. Certain that it had landed in my neighbor's backyard, I climbed the fence, imagining a glowing, five-pointed star lodged in the lawn. I was determined to pluck that star from the ground and place it in a glass jar, where it could light up my room like a celestial night light.

But the yard was dark. No star. I fought back the tears and climbed back down to earth.

Stars aren't meant to be caught and confined in jars. Their power is way beyond such limitations. We can no more trap a star in a jar than we can express in words how it feels to fall in love.

It's like Zechariah trying to put into words what the pending birth of Jesus meant to the world. For nine long months, Zechariah had kept his mouth shut, but not by his own choice. When the angel Gabriel came to the temple to tell him that he and his wife, Elizabeth, would have a long-awaited son, Zechariah expressed his doubt in no uncertain terms. Gabriel, in a huff at Zechariah's dubious reaction to the good news, rendered him mute until the child arrived.

For nine long months, the words built up inside Zechariah like flood waters behind a dam.

When the time came to dedicate his newborn son, Zechariah let it be known that the name of the boy would be "John." While Zechariah's family and friends were struck speechless by this unexpected nomenclature, Zechariah found his own voice reinstated. The flood waters broke, and words poured forth from the old man's mouth as fast as he could form the consonants and vowels.

Just before he ran out of breath, he proclaimed the coming of the Christ, the One for whom his own newly born son would pave the way. These were Zechariah's final words that day: "By the tender mercy of our God, the dawn from on high will break upon us, to give light to those who sit in darkness and in the shadow of death, to guide our feet into the way of peace" (Luke 1:78–79).

The dawn from on high will break upon us and spill upon the earth like liquid stars, finding its way into the cracks and crevices of darkness that no earthly light can reach.

Such joy cannot be contained, no more than a star can be held captive in a jar. It's not meant for one person to hoard.

Such light—such joy—such peace—is meant for the whole world to see.

DAY 6

"Hope has nothing to do with optimism. Its opposite is not pessimism but despair. And if Jesus never allowed his soul to be cornered into despair, clearly we Christians shouldn't either."

—William Sloane Coffin, *Credo*, 19

DAY 7

Breath Prayer: Close your eyes; take several slow, deep breaths; then silently pray this breath prayer in rhythm with your breathing. Repeat several times.

Guide my feet
in the way of peace.

— Light your Sabbath Celebration candle. Sit quietly for five minutes.
— Read the Bible passage for this week: Luke 1:78–79.
— Quietly reflect on images of dawn: the sun beginning to rise . . . the colors of the sky, the trees, the land, and the water, as the light grows in intensity . . . the darkness fading. Feel the warmth of the light on your face and back. Enjoy this "internal" sunrise!
— Are there places of darkness in your life? Are there shadows that dim the brightness of the light? What do you think of when you think of "the tender mercy of our God?"
— In your journal, write down the areas in your life where you feel light and joy, the areas that seem to be in shadow, and how the "tender mercy of God" reaches to you in both the light and the dark.
— Pray for God to shine light in the darkness, and for those who are in darkness to be comforted by the promises of Jesus.

The meaning of the Sabbath is to celebrate time rather than space. Six days a week we live under the tyranny of things of space; on the Sabbath we try to become attuned to holiness in time. *(Abraham Joshua Heschel, 10)*

WEEK 3

DAY 1

Read the following Bible passage each day this week:
Psalm 139:1–6.

> O LORD, you have searched me and known me.
> You know when I sit down and when I rise up;
>   you discern my thoughts from far away.
> You search out my path and my lying down,
>   and are acquainted with all my ways.
> Even before a word is on my tongue,
>   O LORD, you know it completely.
> You hem me in, behind and before,
>   and lay your hand upon me.
> Such knowledge is too wonderful for me;
>   it is so high that I cannot attain it.

Spirit Booster: Reaching In
What is one trait that you dislike most about yourself?
God knows all about it and still loves you.

Spirit Booster: Reaching Out
Write down a trait that you dislike in someone else, then
tear it up, and try to see that person through God's eyes.

DAY 2
Inside Out

Our church runs a Christian preschool during the week-days, from September through May. The first week of the new semester, the teachers bring the children to the office so that they can meet those of us who work in the church. One by one, we introduce ourselves, telling the children our names. Then, one by one, the children tell us theirs. One time, a little girl, overcome with shyness, crouched down behind another child and covered her face with her hands. If *she* couldn't see *us*, she figured, then *we* couldn't see *her*, which makes perfect sense in the realm of a young child.

You don't have to be four years old to have the same kind of mind-set. Maybe if I hide my faults, nobody will see them. Maybe if I pretend other people aren't there, they'll just go away. Maybe, just maybe, if we do our best to hide from God, God won't see us and the parts of our lives we'd rather not talk about.

The author of Psalm 139 tells us otherwise: "O LORD, you have searched me and known me. You know when I sit down and when I rise up. . . . Even before a word is on my tongue, O LORD, you know it completely." Indeed, says the psalmist, God knows us even better than we know ourselves. We can't hide from God, any more than Adam and Eve could make themselves invisible with those ridiculous fig leaves they tried to use for camouflage; any more than a three-year-old can hide behind her upraised palms.

Whoever wrote the Christmas song "Santa Claus Is Coming to Town" must have been inspired by Psalm 139. In fact, it could be renamed "Psanta's Psalm":

He sees you when you're sleeping.
He knows when you're awake.
He knows if you've been bad or good,
So be good for goodness' sake!

I don't know about you, but that song always gave me the shivers. I really don't care to have someone watching my every move, waiting for me to commit some minor infraction so that my name will get crossed off the list. I like my privacy! I don't want anyone—Santa or God or whoever else—spying on me. There are parts of my life I'd like to keep to myself, thank you very much!

It takes a lot of work on our part to hide ourselves from other people, from ourselves, and from God. We cover up our thoughts and actions, hoping nobody will notice us. As if God can't see us behind our fig leaves of denial and indecision.

God knows our every motivation, our every thought, our every action, our every neglect. God knows us better than we know ourselves. God knows us inside out.

What is your reaction to the awful, awe-ful truth that God knows everything about you? Terror? Indignation? Shame? The author of Psalm 139 offers another reaction to this incredible knowingness of God: "Such knowledge is too wonderful for me, it is so high I cannot attain it." Too *wonderful*, not too frightening. Too *wonderful*, not too invasive. Too *wonderful*, not too disgraceful.

God knows us, inside out, and it is wonderful, so wonderful we cannot fully understand. We don't need to be frightened fugitives behind fig leaves. The knowledge that God knows us inside out is meant to set us free.

God knows us, warts and all, and still loves us. God knows us, inside out, and still loves us. We can't escape that love! No matter where we go or what we do or who we are, we cannot hide from the fact that *God loves us!* It's as simple—and as unbelievable—as that.

DAY 3
prayer

look at this, she said,
and she held up the baby gate
with missing feet
she found leaning against a garbage can
outside a neighbor's house.

this will be perfect, she said,
for my grandkids:
gorgeous little toddler boys
who visit from time to time.
in fact, they were living with us for a while,
along with our son,
their father.

the thing is, she said,
our son has gone missing
and he took the boys;
there's drugs and theft and lying
and we had to kick him out.
we just want the babies back.

and now, look at this, she said,
rattling the gate at me:
i was out walking, and
someone threw this away!
for them it was trash,
but for me it's an act of faith,

and she hurried down the street
with a rickety prayer tucked under her arm.
—MaryAnn McKibben Dana (unpublished)

DAY 4

"Behold, Lord, an empty vessel that needs to be filled. My Lord, fill it. I am weak in the faith; strengthen me. I am cold in love; warm me and make me fervent, that my love may go out to my neighbor. I do not have a strong and firm faith; at times I doubt and am unable to trust you altogether. O Lord, help me. Strengthen my faith and trust in you. In you I have sealed the treasure of all I have. I am poor; you are rich and came to be merciful to the poor. I am a sinner; you are upright. With me, there is an abundance of sin; in you is the fullness of righteousness. Therefore I will remain with you, of whom I can receive, but to whom I may not give."

—Martin Luther, *The One Year Book of Personal Prayer,*
January 8

DAY 5
All God's Fault

"Kaffy, why is your hair white?" Tommy, my four-year-old neighbor, looked up innocently at me with his dark brown eyes. "My grandma has white hair, too," he continued. I smiled.

I thought for a moment about how to answer his question. Why a mother with a four-year-old son herself has hair like his grandmother. Why someone still in her thirties allows her once-dark hair to go its own way. I thought about quoting my favorite Proverb: "Gray hair is a crown of glory; it is gained in a righteous life" (Proverbs 16:31), but decided that a dose of theology wasn't quite appropriate.

My own young son came to my rescue. "Because God made it that way, right, Mom?" His response was serious, and I tried to treat it as such. The two boys stared at me, then giggled. "Right, David," I finally managed. "Because God made it that way."

How nice it would be if we looked at the world with such an attitude. How marvelous to wake up and breathe the morning air and survey the vast sky, or climb into bed after one last glance at the stars sprinkled across the velvet night and think, "Thanks, God, for making the world this way."

Just as important is the need for each of us to say, in all honesty, "Thanks, God, for making me this way." In our society, where physical beauty, thinness, and glamour pervade our thoughts from the time we first open our eyes at birth, it doesn't take long for us to get caught in the trap that our appearance is the most important part of who we are. And then, instead of thanking God for the gifts that come from deep inside of us—gifts of compassion, concern, generosity—we bury those gifts beneath a facade and concentrate on what's on the outside, not the inside.

We should take care of ourselves, exercise, eat healthy foods, and get enough sleep. But God wants us to take care of our nonvisible gifts with just as much concern. It's great to tell our children, "You look beautiful today," but let's not forget to also say, "It was beautiful the way you shared that toy with your brother." Encourage their inner beauty as well as their outer.

Maybe it's silly, but I think that in some small way, by not coloring my hair, I'm telling my children it's okay for me to be who I am, and it's okay for them to be who they are. Yes, Tommy, my hair is white. It's nothing to be ashamed of. In fact, I rather like it. After all, God made me this way.

DAY 6

"If you do not hope, you will not find out what is beyond your hopes."
—Clement of Alexandria, *The Westminster Collection of Christian Quotations*, 177

DAY 7

Breath Prayer: Close your eyes; take several slow, deep breaths; then silently pray this breath prayer in rhythm with your breathing. Repeat several times.

You search me, Lord,
and you know me.

— Light your Sabbath Celebration candle. Sit quietly for five minutes.
— Read the Bible passage for this week: Psalm 139:1–6.
— Quietly reflect on how God reaches out to you when you are sitting, when you are lying down, when you rise up, when God seems far away, when you are on the road, before you speak, when you speak, behind you, in front of you, all around you.
— The psalmist writes that God "hem[s] me in." Imagine God lovingly stitching the ragged edges of your life and making them smooth, and building a safe structure around you to keep you safe.
— In your journal, write down what God knows about you that seems beyond your understanding. What makes you "tick"?

— Pray to be at peace with your shortcomings, give thanks for your strengths, and know that God hears your prayers, both spoken and unspoken.

Every seventh day a miracle comes to pass, the resurrection of the soul. (Abraham Joshua Heschel, 83)

WEEK 4

DAY 1

Read the following Bible passage each day this week: Hebrews 11:1.

Now faith is the assurance of things hoped for, the conviction of things not seen.

Spirit Booster: Reaching In
Identify one "hope" you have right now. Substitute that "hope" in the Scripture phrase, "Now faith is the assurance of _____, the conviction of things not seen."

Spirit Booster: Reaching Out
Identify a hope you have for someone else—something that will make that person's life better—and pray for that person each day this week.

DAY 2
Sow What?

One morning they weren't there; the next they were.
Seemingly from nowhere they appeared, clusters of

tiny sprouts, twenty or more per group, rising amidst the petunias and pansies, and under the children's play set. I hadn't planted them, this much I knew. What they were or what they would become, I hadn't the slightest idea.

They seemed almost magical, these seedlings. I couldn't help but be impressed by the way they huddled together, merging from uncertain origin. It didn't seem right to me to pull them up like weeds and toss them in the compost pile. They deserved better than that.

I dug them up and transplanted them in neat rows in my garden. Most of them survived, although a few wilted during the transaction and never quite recovered. The majority of them sprang back to life as soon as they drank the rain, and they firmly rooted themselves in the dark, moist soil.

Their growth amazed me. Within weeks, the stalks thickened and stretched toward the summer sun. No sign of any flowers to make them attractive. I nonetheless decided to let them be.

For all I knew they were nothing more than a lot of pesky weeds, fooling me into giving them space so they could throttle the flowers I had intentionally planted. Enchanted by their tenacity, I allowed them to maintain their position among the zinnias and marigolds, kept them watered, and waited.

By mid-August, my faith in these anonymous seedlings was rewarded. Topping the strong, leafy stalks, huge buds began to unfold, tight fists that slowly released their golden fingers and extended their hands in greeting. Sunflowers! Those tiny, curious clusters turned into tall, glorious sunflowers, providing not only beauty for the eye and pollen for the bees but food for the birds. Every morning I checked their progress, thankful that I had given them a chance to survive.

God's faith in us is like my faith in those sunflowers. While we are sprouting, growing, and changing, long before we reach our full potential (if we ever really do), God has faith in us, clearing space in the garden, tending to our growth, watching in wonder, and waiting, always waiting, for us to bloom.

I let a lot of unusual seedlings grow now. Some turn into weeds; some, into beautiful flowers. I figure, why not give them all a chance?

DAY 3
Hope

It hovers in dark corners
before the lights are turned on,
 it shakes sleep from its eyes
 and drops from mushroom gills,
  it explodes in the starry heads
  of dandelions turned sages,
   it sticks to the wings of green angels
   that sail from the tops of maples.

It sprouts in each occluded eye
of the many-eyed potato,
 it lives in each earthworm segment
 surviving cruelty,
  it is the motion that runs
  from the eyes to the tail of a dog,
   it is the mouth that inflates the lungs
   of the child that has just been born.

It is the singular gift
we cannot destroy in ourselves,
the argument that refutes death,
the genius that invents the future,
all we know of God.

It is the serum which makes us swear
not to betray one another;
it is in this poem trying to speak.

—Lisel Mueller, *Alive Together*, 103

DAY 4

O God, our Father, we know our own weakness and we
    know your power. And this day we take
    Our helplessness to your strength;
    Our ignorance to your wisdom;
    Our sin to your purity;
    Our need to your love.

We cannot decide aright what we should do;
    Grant us the guidance which will save us from all
    mistakes.

We cannot conquer our temptations;
    Grant us the grace which can make us clean and keep
    us clean.

We cannot bear the toil of life;
    Grant us the strength to pass the breaking-point and
    not to break.

We cannot escape the worry of life;
    Grant us the peace that passes understanding,
        which the world cannot give or ever take away.

We cannot face the responsibilities of life;
    Grant us to know that there is nothing that we have to
    face alone.

We cannot solve the problems of life;
   Grant us in your wisdom to find the answers
      to the questions which perplex our ignorance.

We cannot find the right way;
   Grant that at every cross-roads of life your Spirit may
      be there to direct us.

We cannot face life alone;
   Grant us to remember that our Lord is with us always
      to the end of the world and beyond.

We cannot face death alone;
   Grant us to be very sure that nothing in life or in
      death,
      can separate us from your love in Christ Jesus our
      Lord.

We come to you for strength in life and for hope when
   life is ended; through Jesus Christ our Lord. Amen.
      —William Barclay, *A Barclay Prayer Book,* 106–107

DAY 5
Glass-Bottom Boats

Whenever family from out of town came to visit us in
southern California where I grew up, we served as willing
tour guides. As kids, we thought this was great! We got to
go to Disneyland and Knotts Berry Farm and Universal
Studios. One of our favorite sightseeing destinations was
the island of Catalina, about twenty miles from the main-
land. On a clear day, we could see the outline of Catalina
shimmering in the distance like a wondrous mirage. The
journey across the stretch of ocean held its own wonders:

flying fish, dolphins, even an occasional whale. My brother and I discovered that if you dropped a piece of paper over the side of the steamship in just the right place, it would whirl up into the sky only to be sucked into one of the smokestacks on the ship, which sent us into peals of laughter at our clever little trick.

Once on Catalina Island, we did the usual touristy things. We always made sure to take a ride on a glass-bottom boat. The wooden floors of the boats had been replaced with thick panels of glass. Benches ringed the perimeter of the glass, and we sat on the edge of those benches, peering carefully over the railing that kept us in our seats.

The boats motored out of the harbor to where the waters were more settled. The navigators then cut the engines, and the boats glided silently along.

Within minutes, brightly colored fish swam into view. We watched them weave in between rippling strands of seaweed, oblivious to our presence. For half an hour, we gaped at the bounteous ocean life right before our eyes, life that we never would have known even existed if it weren't for the glass-bottom boats that allowed us to see what was right there all long. Before we knew it, our half-hour tour finished, and the boats cranked up their engines and carried us back to dry land.

Faith is like those glass-bottom boats. There's so much wonder and beauty all around us. Faith helps us to look at the world a little more clearly, to see the life that is right there before us, life that we miss if we don't take our boats into deeper water, turn off the engines, wait, and watch. Faith helps us to see beyond the dark, murky waters, to a place of hope that lies within our reach, and not so far away as we may at times think.

So often we miss what is just beyond our field of vision: the eggs in the nest, nestled under a protective mother bird; the rainbow fish teeming beneath the calm surface of the water; the gentle gaze of someone who loves us; the noise and colors and commotion that bless our lives.

It's all right there, a gift from God. Faith encourages us to believe in what we cannot see, because every now and then, we are blessed with the vision of the glass-bottom boats, and catch a glimpse into the wonderful world of God's creation.

DAY 6

"There is treasure buried in the field of every one of our days, even the bleakest or dullest, and it is our business, as we journey, to keep our eyes peeled for it."
—Frederick Buechner, *The Longing for Home*, 120

DAY 7

Breath Prayer: Close your eyes; take several slow, deep breaths; then silently pray this breath prayer in rhythm with your breathing. Repeat several times.

> *Lord, give me faith
> and grant me hope.*

— Light your Sabbath Celebration candle. Sit quietly for five minutes.
— Read the Bible passage for this week: Hebrews 11:1.
— Quietly reflect on the word "hope." How does it feel to have hope? What gives you hope?
— "Conviction" implies a powerful assurance. What beliefs do you feel most strongly about?
— In your journal, write down what "assurance" means to

you. How do you use this word in reference to your faith?

— Pray for hope in times of uncertainty, and trust in what you cannot see.

It was on the seventh day that the world was given a soul. (Abraham Joshua Heschel, 83)

JUNE
SPIRIT

WEEK 1

DAY 1

Read the following Bible passage each day this week: Genesis 1:1–3.

> In the beginning when God created the heavens and the earth, the earth was a formless void and darkness covered the face of the deep, while a wind from God swept over the face of the waters.

Spirit Booster: Reaching In
If you live near a body of water—a lake, ocean, stream, river, or pond—spend some quiet time watching the water. Notice how it changes color, how the surface can be still or moving, how it sounds. If you do not live near water, find photos or drawings of water in books or magazines and enjoy!

Spirit Booster: Reaching Out
Be aware of the ways you waste water: letting the faucet run while you brush your teeth or rinse dishes, spending a long time in the shower or filling the bathtub full every day, watering outside plants when it is hot and much of the water evaporates. Try to cut back on the waste, remembering that water is a precious resource and that, for many people in the world, it is scarce or hard to find.

DAY 2
Summer Snow

The community where I live is built around a lake. The houses, once consisting solely of summertime homes, have gradually expanded and filled the winding streets. Grand new homes take their place alongside dwellings that were born as humble cabins. The acres surrounding this community are rapidly becoming overrun with new housing developments that stretch in every direction.

One thing in particular sets my community apart from all those fancy complexes: the trees. In all the new communities, there are few, if any, trees. The ones that have been planted are small and frail. But in Wildwood, trees abound. Majestic oaks and maples shelter homes and yards, providing welcome shade in the summer and piles of flame-colored leaves in the fall, much to the delight of children and the chagrin of those who rake. Graceful evergreens provide splashes of color in the bleakness of winter, and when the snow first falls, the green needles are iced with white frosting that turns the entire neighborhood into a fairyland. Springtime brings new life as buds and leaves unfurl and blossom and fill the world with hope.

Each morning as I walk, I drink in the trees. I marvel at their thick, rough trunks and powerful roots breaking through the earth. Branches are as diverse as hands, some slender and smooth, others crooked and gnarled. They lift my eyes up off the ground and direct my attention to a broader empire. We are friends, the trees and I.

One early morning I walked my usual path, around the lake and down a quiet street. As I turned the bend, something in the air caught my eye. A snowflake, then another, then dozens more, floating silently on a gentle breeze. Soon the air filled with delicate white puffs. Stunned, I reached out and caught one in my hand. My surprise came not from the snow, for I have seen this beauty before. But this was a Saturday morning in June, and the air far too warm for winter folly.

The snow, as it turned out, was not made of icy crystals but cottonwood seeds. A tree somewhere, or perhaps two or three, had given birth to thousands of offspring, tiny seeds, carried by tufts of cotton parachutes to varied destinations. One lawn, blanketed in white, appeared to be the maternity ward of the cottonwoods. I stopped walking and stood in the midst of this summer snowfall, enveloped in nature's gift, seeds of new life, new beginnings.

As I went my way, I pondered what had at first appeared to be a miracle but had turned out to be only a common act of nature. Then I stopped, and glancing back across my shoulder at the air still freckled with white, I wondered: Are fragile tufted cottonwood seeds rising and falling on the breath of the morning any less a miracle of God than snowflakes in June?

(Previously published in *Voice of Many Waters*,
Snodgrass, ed., 15–16)

DAY 3

Your Spirit, O Creator God,
your brooding, bright, imagining Spirit,
has brought us —
and all that was, and is, and ever shall be —
has brought us into being.

Your Spirit, O Creator God,
your brooding, bright imagining Spirit,
has called us beyond being,
has huffed and puffed, tugged and shoved,
has kneaded and molded us beyond being into life.

Your Spirit, O Creator God,
your brooding, bright imagining Spirit,
is inviting us, cajoling us, entrancing, inducing,
yes, even seducing us, beyond life into creation,
into imagination, into all the shapes and hues,
the textures, postures, melodies of grace.

So let that flaming, flagrant Spirit
be afire now among us here.
Lift our imaginations through the laughter of the soul.
Restore to us our poetic vision,
that we may see this world anew
as your mighty work-in-progress,
that we may see ourselves as others see us,
that we may see you, the unseen God,
as the source and goal and heart of all delight.

Through these moments of welcoming,
of sustenance, of encouragement, mirth and wisdom,
move up, across, among us once again
with your Spirit of inspiration and of ecstasy.

We ask this in the name of the living Word,
that Word we seek and find and lose,
and then are found by.
Let us say . . . AMEN.

       —J. Barrie Shepherd (unpublished)

DAY 4
To make things new that never were

We name you wind, power, force, and then,
   imaginatively, "Third Person."
We name you and you blow . . .

blow hard,
blow cold,
blow hot,
blow strong,
blow gentle,
blow new . . .
Blowing the world out of nothing to abundance,
blowing the church out of despair to new life,
blowing little David from shepherd boy to messiah,
blowing to make things new that never were.
So blow this day, wind,
blow here and there, power,
blow even us, force,
Rush us beyond ourselves,
Rush us beyond our hopes,
Rush us beyond our fears, until we enact your newness
in the world.
Come, come spirit. Amen.
—Walter Brueggemann, *Awed to Heaven,*
Rooted in Earth, 167

<hr>

DAY 5
When the Wind Blows

In the beginning when God created the heavens and
the earth, the earth was a formless void and darkness covered the face of the deep, while a wind from
God swept over the face of the waters. . . .

I've seen the wind sweep over the face of the waters. We
live on a small lake, so it's not an unusual site. It's beautiful, in fact.

When I think of the wind sweeping across the waters, I
think of movement like a hand sweeping crumbs from a

table. The wind sweeps the lake from one end to the other, then continues on its way in a great, big hurry.

The Hebrew word used in the passage from Genesis includes more than just a sweeping movement. The wind "hovers" and "broods." That isn't a quick, fleeting movement at all. Hovering and brooding brings images of pausing or thinking or contemplating. "Brooding" makes it sound like the wind had a lot of options to consider, some more appealing than others.

I like that. The wind—the Spirit—sweeps, hovers, broods. Creation takes time. Creation takes thought. Creation takes some sorting out, some decision making.

That fits the concept of creation springing up from the "Word." Kind of like creative writing. God creates the world through the Word—not a single word shouted out here and there, like a toddler learning to identify objects: "Tree!" "Spoon!" "Up!" More like an essay, perhaps, a creative thinking through of words, a brooding over definitions and phrases. The lake isn't just "blue." It shimmers like liquid sapphires. The wind hovers, the Spirit broods, the Word speaks in a poignant, powerful paragraph of possibilities.

Sweeping. Hovering. Brooding. The final product—the heavens and the earth in all their glory—leaves us, well, speechless.

DAY 6

"Like its counterparts in Hebrew and Greek, the Latin word *spiritus* originally meant "breath" (as in *expire, respiratory,* and so on), and breath is what you have when you're alive and don't have when you're dead. Thus spirit = breath = life, the aliveness and power of your life, and to speak of your spirit (or soul) is to speak of the power of

life that is in you. When your spirit is unusually strong, the life in you unusually alive, you can breathe it out into other lives, become literally in-spiring."
—Frederick Buechner, *Beyond Words*, 375–76

DAY 7

Breath Prayer: Close your eyes; take several slow, deep breaths; then silently pray this breath prayer in rhythm with your breathing. Repeat several times.

> *In the beginning,*
> *you created, O God.*

— Light your Sabbath Celebration candle. Sit quietly for five minutes.
— Read the Bible passage for this week: Genesis 1:1–3.
— Quietly reflect on the images of void: darkness, the face of the deep, a wind sweeping over water. Which images are most powerful for you?
— The Scripture states that "a wind from God swept over the waters." What kind of wind do you think it was? Forceful like a tornado or a hurricane? A summer breeze that ripples the surface of the water? A swirling wind? A wind that blows steadily or sporadically? What kinds of sound does the wind make?
— In your journal, describe the kinds of wind you like best. Soft and gentle? Brisk and cold? Explain why.
— Pray for the Spirit to sweep across your soul, like the wind over the waters of creation.

The Sabbath is not holy by the grace of [humankind]. It was God who sanctified the seventh day. (Abraham Joshua Heschel, 76)

WEEK 2

DAY 1

Read the following Bible passage each day this week: John 14:25–27.

> "I have said these things to you while I am still with you. But the Advocate, the Holy Spirit, whom the Father will send in my name, will teach you every-thing, and remind you of all that I have said to you. Peace I leave with you; my peace I give to you. I do not give to you as the world gives. Do not let your hearts be troubled, and do not let them be afraid."

Spirit Booster: Reaching In
Play some music that soothes your spirit and makes you feel at peace. Do not do anything else but LISTEN!

Spirit Booster: Reaching Out
Some churches have a time of "passing the peace of Christ" to the people sitting around you. Try passing the peace of Christ to a family member or a friend. Tell that person that you wish for the peace of Christ to be in his or her life.

DAY 2
Keep Trying

I'm flying west to visit my parents. My mother is sick. My mind is fried. My flight is delayed.

I have to change planes in Los Angeles. Although I grew up in the L.A. area, there is no sentimental nostalgia as I walk off the plane into the terminal. I am greeted by a woman with a plastic container, collecting money for a shelter for abused women. She grabs me with her eyes and launches into her spiel. I hesitate. I don't want to throw my money away. Even though she has an "official" name tag, I am not sure if she is legitimate. I stuff a dollar into her container, not willing to part with the twenty dollar bills which are the only other bills I have. She thanks me, and I turn and wander into a candy shop. I buy some treats for my parents. Then I feel guilty at spending seven bucks in a candy store when I hesitated to give $1.00 to a women's shelter. I take the change and go to find the woman and make amends. But she is long gone.

Moments later, as I drag my carry-on luggage to the gate where I will catch the next plane, I hear a voice over the loudspeaker: "Attention travelers. Please maintain visual contact with your possessions at all times. Do not leave your bags unattended." There is a pause, and the voice continues, "You are not required to give money to solicitors. This airport does not sponsor their activities." I think of the vanished woman. Was she some fraud? Or Jesus in disguise? Probably someone in between the two extremes, just like all of us.

Living by the Spirit, and being guided by the Spirit, isn't as easy as Galatians makes it sound, even when we have good intentions, and mean to do the right thing, and want to believe that our actions and deeds are motivated by faith. When it comes right down to it, we're all going to make mistakes and not know it. We are all going to do the right thing, and not know that either.

I will never know if the woman collecting money at the airport was legitimate or not. I can't go back and change how I reacted. I give generously of my money and time, and I will do so again to many charities, and strangers, I am sure of that.

Maybe I'm just fooling myself, but perhaps buying my parents a little treat is how God intended for me to spend my money that day. I will just have to keep trying to do my best, to live by the Spirit each and every day.

DAY 3
Communion

Gently—like rain on a spring-warm day—
    the words fell
        into my face,
    splashing, rolling, embedding
        in the burrows of my being:
THE BLESSINGS OF CHRIST BE WITH YOU.
There in the midst of broken bread
    in a world of broken bodies
        and splintered spirits
the communion of saints
    became new again,
washed once more
    in blessing and promise.
        —Ann Weems, *Searching for Shalom*, 42

DAY 4

O God, our Father, we remember that Jesus promised
   that he would send to us the Holy Spirit from you.
   Keep that promise to us today.
He called his Spirit the Spirit of truth.
   Open our eyes that we may see the truth;
   Strengthen our hearts that we may face the truth;
   Enlighten our minds that we may understand the truth;
   Make our memories retentive that we may remember
      the truth;
   Make resolute our wills that we may obey the truth,
      through the Spirit which he has promised us.

Amen.

— William Barclay, *A Barclay Prayer Book,* 84

DAY 5
An Unexpected Comfort

My mother was always a practical woman. During the
year she fought lung cancer, she maintained that quality.
Never knowing if she would end up suddenly in the emergency room or the hospital, she kept extra clothes in her
van. I don't think she ever used the clothes (ones she had,
as always, sewn herself), but I remember seeing them
when I'd be visiting, unloading a bag of groceries or taking her overnight bag to the hospital.

Several months after Mom died, my husband, our kids,
and I flew to Las Vegas to spend time with my father and
to meet up with Greg's family for a reunion. We needed a

way to get from Vegas to Lake Powell. My dad loaned us his van so that we could cart a load of luggage and swim gear, not to mention a few extra niceties. We had that van so full of stuff that there was little room left for the passengers, but we managed to squeeze in and headed north to meet with the rest of the family.

We had the air conditioning on, because it was, after all, August in Nevada, and the weather verified this. An hour or two into the trip, I started getting chilly, sitting by the window in the middle section of the van, a few cold air vents blowing across my capri-clad legs. I glanced sideways into the back of the van, seeking a spare jacket or something with which I could cover my legs. I saw what I thought was my daughter's blue velour top and figured that would work fine. I grabbed it and pulled it forward to my seat and started to spread it across my legs.

It wasn't Amy's top. It took me a few minutes to realize that I held an elastic-waisted pair of blue velour slacks in my hands. My mother's slacks, left there in the back of the van all these months after her death, and not even noticed when we loaded up all our stuff.

I smoothed the soft material across my lap and shed quiet tears. I felt again the deep loss of my mother's death. Yet through the tears and the ache of my heart, I had to smile. It was just like my mother to make sure that I was cared for, kept warm, comforted. That old pair of slacks, tossed aside in the van, connected me to my mother's undying love.

When Jesus speaks of the Holy Spirit as "the Comforter," I imagine a warm, gentle Spirit wrapping us in arms of love. I imagine feeling the peace I felt with those velour slacks draped over my lap.

When we least expect it, God finds a way to reach into our lives and bring comfort.

DAY 6

"The spiritual life invites a process of transformation in the life of a believer. It is a process of growing in gratitude, trust, obedience, humility, compassion, service, and joy."
— Marjorie Thompson, *Soul Feast, 7*

DAY 7

Breath Prayer: Close your eyes; take several slow, deep breaths; then silently pray this breath prayer in rhythm with your breathing. Repeat several times.

Let not my heart be troubled;
do not let me be afraid.

— Light your Sabbath Celebration candle. Sit quietly for five minutes.
— Read the Bible passage for this week: John 14:25–27.
— Quietly reflect on the calming words of Jesus to the disciples when they were afraid. Repeat several times, "Do not let my heart be troubled, and do not let me be afraid."
— Jesus refers to the Holy Spirit as the "Advocate." An advocate is someone who serves on your behalf, who has your best interests in mind, and who is willing to defend you. Have you thought of the Holy Spirit in this way? In what ways has the Holy Spirit been an Advocate in your life?
— In your journal, write down the thoughts that are troubling your heart. After each thought, add the words,

"Do not let my heart be troubled; do not let me be afraid."

— Pray for the Advocate, the Holy Spirit, to keep you from troubling thoughts and fear.

The seventh day is the exodus from tension. (Abraham Joshua Heschel, 29)

WEEK 3

DAY 1

Read the following Bible passage each day this week: Psalm 63:1–4.

> O God, you are my God, I seek you,
>   my soul thirsts for you; my flesh faints for you,
>   as in a dry and weary land where there is no water.
> So I have looked upon you in the sanctuary,
>   beholding your power and glory.
> Because your steadfast love is better than life,
>   my lips will praise you.
> So I will bless you as long as I live;
>   I will lift up my hands and call on your name.

Spirit Booster: Reaching In
Count your blessings. Name them and give thanks to God.

Spirit Booster: Reaching Out
Think about the people at your church who clean and take care of the sanctuary so that it can be a place of worship, a place to behold God's glory. Call and thank someone, or send a card, saying that you appreciate the work they do that often goes unrecognized.

DAY 2
Water for the Soul

It is a March day in 2004. One of my mother's brothers has died in California, and I am presiding at the funeral. I fly to Las Vegas, where my father lives, and there meet another uncle who lives in Florida.

My father, uncle, and I drive to California from Las Vegas, crossing over the desert for much of the way. The scenery is so different from back home in Wildwood, where there are still splotches of snow carpeting the earth. Here in the desert, everything is dry, dry, dry. I see some very large puddles along the road in places, not so much a sign of the rains that passed through here last week but more a stark reminder that the ground itself is so dry and hard that, even when it does rain, the water cannot sink through the crust.

Our souls are like that, I think. Sometimes so hardened and dry that even the living water of Christ struggles to pierce the shell we have allowed to form. When our spirits are contained within such an unreachable place, it is only drop by drop that the water manages to seep through the tiniest of cracks.

The desert has adapted to its dry climate. The vegetation—cactus and other native plants—have found a way to survive and even flourish. Plants that grow on desert ground know how to preserve the water that is scarce. Maybe when we feel parched and dry, our spirits, too, survive by carefully portioning out the living water that is there, that living water of Christ that causes beauty to bloom even in our desert days.

O God, you are my God, I seek you,
   my soul thirsts for you;
my flesh faints for you,
   as in a dry and weary land where there is no water.

(Ps. 63:1)

King David wrote this psalm when he was in a desert place: his once glorious kingdom was split by power and greed, and his beloved son was stabbed and left hanging in a tree to die. Talk about your whole life falling apart. Talk about living in a spiritual desert.

David is in the desert, longing to return to a place of sanctuary and peace and blessing. He knows that God has not abandoned him, but he yearns to get back to that oasis of joy where his thirst for God is quenched: "I have looked upon you in the sanctuary, beholding your power and glory."

David is in the desert.

I know the feeling.

We finally get through the desert of Nevada and pass into the land of California, the land of my birth, my childhood, my adolescence. I yearn to see the Pacific Ocean again—it has been far too many years since I gazed at its beauty and vastness. We will be staying at a hotel only two blocks away from the ocean, so I am sure I will see it. The ocean always did have a way of soothing my soul.

But there is not enough time. Between preparing for the funeral and running back and forth between my aunt's house and the hotel, there just isn't time.

Instead, I get to visit with aunts, uncles, and cousins I haven't seen in years. We remember years long ago and the times spent visiting. My beloved brother is able to be with us. We laugh together, and it is good. I get to meet my cousin's baby, whom I've never seen before.

I have unexpected time with my father, on the drive to California and then back to Vegas. These are sweet blessings that fall like rain upon my weary soul.

I never did get over to see the Pacific Ocean, but that turned out to be okay. The ocean will always be there. The time I spent with family was what I really needed anyway. I'm sure God knew that all along.

DAY 3
a poem in 300 seconds

i noticed something the other
day driving in the car —
looking through the rear-view mirror —
superimposed on the traffic
(trailing, passing, flashing)
was my little girl,
but she wasn't all there, she was
see-through like a ghost.
and the light had to be just right
otherwise she vanished,
or i just saw an arm,
or the dark outline of her carseat buckle,
or the glint of blond hair.
even with her whole transparent face
framed in that lopsided rectangle
i didn't like the view.
because she is no spirit
haunting me over my shoulder.
she is real,
clapping quiet hands
singing a song without words
peering out the window like i'm
driving miss daisy.
i'd rather see her
so i flip the mirror
down into the other position,
and she's solid again
and she can see me!
and now it's everyone else
who flashes in and out of view,
a phantom world.
> —MaryAnn McKibben Dana
> (unpublished)

DAY 4

"Teach us, O God not to torture ourselves, not to make martyrs of ourselves through stifling reflection; but rather teach us to breathe deeply in faith, through Jesus, our Lord."
— Søren Kierkegaard, *The Complete Book of Christian Prayer*, 206

DAY 5
Beneath the Surface

There was life in the lake this morning. It has always been there, I know. But today it became apparent in a way I have never seen before.

On most days, life seems only to exist above the horizon of water. The mirror surface of the lake mimics the mood of the sky, reflecting the images of trees that balance along the edges of the shore, admiring themselves and dipping their toes in the cool water. At other times, the frisky breezes tickle the surface until it ripples with laughter. The water appears one-dimensional, a vast blue carpet stretching between the shores, a dividing line separating the life above and the nothingness below.

Until this morning. As I walked quickly along the edge of the road, I heard a sound I hadn't heard before. My puzzled gaze was drawn to the shallow inlet beyond an empty lot. Something moved about in the water. I crept closer to the edge, stepping cautiously so as not to frighten the cause of this curious disruption.

The culprit was a large school of fish, twisting and rolling, flipping and thrashing until the small section of dark water resembled a bubbling pit of lava. I was captivated. I didn't care what the fish were doing. I found myself struck by the fact that there was so much life beneath the surface.

Isn't that true about life above the surface? The life we see every day and hardly notice? Look around! See the trees that stand barren and stark in the winter: buds and leaves will reappear in the spring and remind us that there's life beneath the surface. Look around! See the old man who sits shrunken and silent in the wheelchair, a shadow of his vibrant past: there's life beneath the surface. Look around! See the awkward teenage girl, who shyly watches peers oblivious to her existence. Can't you see, there's life beneath the surface. Look around, look close by. There's life beneath the surface, if we care enough to notice.

For such is the love God has for us: to know our very depths, to know the secrets of our hearts, to know our thoughts and feelings and failings and triumphs, and to love us for what lies below the surface, not above. To be known and understood so deeply, and to be loved so richly, are truly gifts from God. Perhaps we would do better to love others and even love ourselves as God loves us — not for our exteriors but for who we really are in our innermost depths.

Our souls thirst to be known by the One who, amidst great power and glory, loves us with a love that will never die, a love that death could not conquer.

Tomorrow morning, the lake will be still once again. But that's okay. I know now that there's life beneath the surface.

<hr>

DAY 6

"Scripturally speaking, the spiritual life is simply the increasing vitality and sway of God's Spirit in us. It is a magnificent choreography of the Holy Spirit in the human spirit, moving us toward communion with both Creator and creation."

— Marjorie Thompson, *Soul Feast*, 6

DAY 7

Breath Prayer: Close your eyes; take several slow, deep breaths; then silently pray this breath prayer in rhythm with your breathing. Repeat several times.

I seek you, O God;
my soul thirsts for you.

— Light your Sabbath Celebration candle. Sit quietly for five minutes.
— Read the Bible passage for this week: Psalm 63:1–4.
— Quietly reflect on the beauty of the sanctuary where you worship. Look carefully at the space around you right now and think of that as a sanctuary of worship as well.
— Have you ever been so thirsty you felt that your mouth was completely dry? Remember how it felt to drink a glass of cold water, to quench your thirst? Think of the Spirit as that which quenches your spirit when you feel dry. What images come to mind?
— In your journal, write and reflect on the times when you felt spiritually dry or drained. What was going on in your life at the time? How did you find refreshment for your Spirit—through prayer, the care of a friend, music?
— Pray to God with words of praise and offer a blessing to God (you can use the line from Psalm 63: "I will bless you as long as I live").

The Sabbath is no time for personal anxiety or care, for
any activity that might dampen the spirit of joy.
(Abraham Joshua Heschel, 30)

WEEK 4

DAY 1

Read the following Bible passage each day this week: Galatians 5:25–26.

> If we live by the Spirit, let us also be guided by the Spirit. Let us not become conceited, competing against one another, envying one another.

Spirit Booster: Reaching In
Jealousy and envy create a sense that you are lacking something that you feel you deserve. Be honest about this. If you feel jealous about what someone else has that you don't have, why is it so important that you have it? Do you really need it? Be aware of any jealous feelings you have and by identifying them, seek to let them go.

Spirit Booster: Reaching Out
If you are jealous of other people's looks, good fortune, or life circumstances, instead of feeling competitive, congratulate them on what it is you admire about them or wish that you had.

DAY 2
As Real as the Air We Breathe

For many people, the story of Pentecost is the defining characteristic of what the Holy Spirit is all about: the violent wind blasting through the windows of a house and igniting the disciples with tongues of flames like fire. The story of Pentecost is one way the Spirit can blow through our lives—but it is not the only way.

After Jesus' baptism, the Spirit appeared in the form of a dove descending from Heaven. The Spirit did not sail out of the heavens in the form of a vulture or a hawk or an ostrich but in the form of a dove. A dove is a gentle bird, and small. It is the symbol for peace as well as for the Holy Spirit. A dove is a very different image of the Spirit than the one of hurricane winds and fire.

In John's gospel, during the Last Supper as Jesus prepares his disciples for his death, he tells them that God will send them an "Advocate," the Spirit of truth. This Spirit will, in Jesus' words, "teach you everything, and remind you of all that I have said to you." The Spirit is an Advocate, one who encourages, upholds, supports, and sustains. The Spirit is not something to be feared, but a friend, a comforter, who teaches us how to be a follower of Jesus.

On the night of Jesus' resurrection, he appeared to the disciples. Frightened, sad, and confused by Mary's declaration that Jesus had risen from the dead, the disciples cowered in a house, locked away in fear. Jesus came to them and said, "Peace be with you." He extended his arms—those arms which, only a few days before had been stretched on the cross, pierced by nails, bleeding—and lets out a deep sigh. Then he breathes on the disciples and says, "Receive the Holy Spirit." The Holy Spirit doesn't knock them off their feet but stands them back up again, so that they can face the world without Jesus and yet in a new way—*with* him—as never before.

The apostle Paul teaches us about the Holy Spirit in many of the books of the New Testament, which are letters that he wrote to brand-new churches. It is the Spirit, writes Paul, that gives us different gifts and abilities. "Now there are varieties of gifts, but the same Spirit," we read in 1 Corinthians 12:4. Everyone is given a "manifestation of the Spirit for the common good." The common good. Paul goes on to say that Christians should "strive to excel in [spiritual gifts] for building up the church" (1 Corinthians 14:12). The gifts of the Spirit are for the common good, for the building up of the church, the body of Christ.

The Spirit gives gifts to use not just for building a healthy church but also for building a healthy self. Paul addresses this in Galatians when he defines the gifts as "fruit"—and I'm not talking apples and oranges. "The fruit of the Spirit," writes Paul, "is love, joy, peace, patience, kindness, generosity, faithfulness, gentleness, and self-control" (Galatians 5:22–23). The Holy Spirit gives us gifts that make us kinder and more compassionate and that allow us to find peace in our spirit when the world dumps all kinds of destructive feelings upon us.

Perhaps the message of Pentecost is that the Spirit speaks all languages as it did on Pentecost. The Spirit speaks in all our languages so that everyone can hear it and understand. The Spirit speaks in the language of a roar and a rush, a whisper and a hush, a cyclone and a cry, a flutter and a sigh.

The Holy Spirit speaks all our languages, and it is as real as . . . well, as real as the air we breathe.

DAY 3

The word *death*
lives deep in the oddly branched vines of the lungs.
It is a wind instrument with no stops, a low
whine you ignore because conversation, or the owl's eye
yellow of the sky at dusk, or the solid crack of wood
split for the fire distract and claim you.

I am learning to breathe
without asking for breath to carry me anywhere
but here, to the split-second rush before wind
strikes word, to the moment I am what I am
without knowing it.

—Margaret Gibson, *Earth Elegy*, from poem,
"Affirmations," 155

DAY 4

Spirit of God,
you are the breath of creation,
the wind of change that blows through our lives,
opening us up to new dreams and new hopes,
new life in Jesus Christ.

Forgive us our closed minds
which barricade themselves against new ideas,
preferring the past to what you might want to do
through us tomorrow.

Forgive our closed eyes
which clutch our gifts and our wealth
for our own use alone.

Forgive us our closed hearts
which limit our affections to ourselves
and our own.

Spirit of new life,
forgive us and break down the prison walls of our
    selfishness,
that we might be open to your love
and open for the service of your world,
through Jesus Christ our Lord.
Amen.

          —Christopher Ellis, *Bread of Tomorrow*, 126

DAY 5
Oxygen Mask

I don't travel as much as a lot of people, whose daily jobs require frequent flying. I have flown enough to have the flight rules memorized. I try to pay attention, but it's hard. I feel as though I've heard the same instructions a million times: "Should there be a change in air pressure, an oxygen mask will drop out of the overhead compartment. . . . Please secure your own oxygen mask before you assist someone else."

This admonition has always sounded strange. Wouldn't we want to help a child or an adult who needed assistance before we attached our own oxygen masks? The problem is, you may run out of air if you do it that way, and then you are no good to anyone, including yourself. You can't help someone else if your own oxygen has run out.

We all—even the pastor—have to take time to put on our own spiritual oxygen masks before we can assist others. We all need breathers now and then, time to allow the Spirit to replenish our spirits. It isn't a luxury to let your spirit breathe. It is absolutely essential, because, if you're not careful, you may run out of air.

When weather permits, I walk. The fresh air surrounds me like the love of a dear friend, always there, always listening. This is my time, alone with the world, and with myself.

The sights are familiar; I see them most every day. Yet I never tire of them. The houses clothed in aluminum siding, the majestic trees stretching out their protective arms, and the flower beds filled with jeweled flowers or flame-colored autumn leaves are new each time I see them. I realize I am smiling as my eyes are drawn to the crisp, clean sky where a flock of geese scatter across the heights as if some divine artist has taken a brush of black ink and flicked it upon a blue canvas. The sound of the geese's rhythmic cries soothes me like a symphony.

A scramble of thoughts scurry through my mind like crisp leaves whipping across the road, blown by a brisk, autumn breeze. The worries and stresses from the past day settle peacefully, leaving room for a fresh supply.

I breathe slowly, and as deeply as possible. My body is refreshed, but so is my spirit. As I walk and breathe, I pray. I pray for the people I know who are struggling. I pray for the world. I thank God for the beauty of the trees and sky and the fresh, boundless air.

Now that my Spirit is filled, I have something to offer the people who need me. The airlines have it right. You have to put on your own oxygen mask first, before you can help the next person.

DAY 6

"Spiritual life depends on the purposes we cherish."
—Charles Haddon Spurgeon, *The Westminster Collection of Christian Quotations*, 360

DAY 7

Breath Prayer: Close your eyes; take several slow, deep breaths; then silently pray this breath prayer in rhythm with your breathing. Repeat several times.

Spirit of God,
lead me and guide me.

— Light your Sabbath Celebration candle. Sit quietly for five minutes.
— Read the Bible passage for this week: Galatians 5:25–26.
— Quietly reflect on the qualities or possessions that you envy in others. Why are these things so important to you?
— Examine your own motives for the way you choose to live. Do you put a lot of importance on appearances and accumulation of material possessions? Do you feel as though no matter what you have, it is never enough? Think about what is truly most important to you.
— In your journal, confess the ways you feel envy or jealousy toward others. By writing them down, you are forced to confront them and to begin the process of moving away from jealousy to joy at the good fortune of other people.
— Pray for God to lead you from jealousy and envy to gratitude and grace.

[The Sabbath] seeks to displace the coveting of things in
space for coveting the things in time. (Abraham
Joshua Heschel, 91)

JULY
LOYALTY

WEEK 1

DAY 1

Read the following Bible passage each day this week: Ruth 1:16–17.

But Ruth said,

> "Do not press me to leave you
>   or to turn back from following you!
> Where you go, I will go;
>   where you lodge, I will lodge;
> your people shall be my people,
>   and your God my God.
> Where you die, I will die —
>   there will I be buried.
> May the LORD do thus and so to me,
>   and more as well,
> if even death parts me from you!"

Spirit Booster: Reaching In
Repeat these words as if God were speaking to you: "Where you go, I will go; where you lodge, I will lodge; your people are my people, and I am your God."

Take time this week to look at old photographs of family, and thank God for each person who is part of your life, even if you have never met.

————————— ∽∽ —————————

DAY 2
The Little Things

When I think of my mom, two things come immediately to mind.

Hand lotion. And tea.

Mom was always on the lookout for a bargain. Her cupboards overflowed with crackers, laundry soap, and soda pop that she and Dad never drank but that she could never pass up at the grocery store because she'd get it for free with all her coupons and bargains.

For years, my mother brought me tubes of hand lotion whenever she came to visit. She'd stock up on tubes she got for free, more than she could use, so she'd bring them to me. Some folks have a never-ending bounty of loaves and fishes. I have a lifetime supply of hand lotion.

And the tea. I never learned to drink coffee, but somewhere along the line, I learned to love tea.

When I left home to attend seminary, the "tradition of the tea" began. Whenever I came back to visit my parents, we would no sooner get in the door of the house than Mom said, "How about a cup of tea?" She'd put on the teakettle and make us tea, and that was our reentry ritual. Now, when my Dad comes to visit, I'm the one making tea, whether it's ninety degrees outside or two o'clock in the morning.

Little things, really. Hand lotion. Tea.

It's the little things that make life so precious. Tucking the blanket under a child's chin so that no amount of tossing and turning will tear it loose. Cutting a peanut butter and jelly sandwich into perfect, equilateral triangles. The scent of vanilla that lingers in the bathrobe, even after it's been hanging in the closet all summer. Little things that carve the nooks and crannies into our souls in a way that can never be duplicated in anyone else.

The Bible doesn't tell us much about the home life that Naomi and Ruth shared before their husbands died. In those days, when a man married, he brought his wife to live with his family. Undoubtedly, Naomi and Ruth worked side by side in the household, cleaning, baking, and talking. Strong bonds formed during those years — bonds that made Ruth decide to stay with Naomi when their husbands died rather than return to her own homeland.

I'll bet it wasn't just sharing the grief of widowhood that bound these two women together. I'll bet it was the little things that happened before all that.

Walking to market, whispering about the vendors and who had the best pomegranates, remembering the time that one fellow at the market made eyes at Ruth one week and Naomi the next. Sitting on the stone wall by the garden; inhaling the cool, night air after a long, hot day spent baking; watching the stars blink good-night. Maybe even preparing tea together before the sun rose in the morning.

It's the little things that bind us close, not just the big ones. Treasure the little moments of this day, this week. Treasure the little things that you share with the people you love. Treasure the little things, for they are what make life so sweet. They are what you may remember most as time goes on.

DAY 3
Faith

A profession of faith is not a part-time promise;
    it's a whole time / all the time / every time way of
       life,
and we who say we believe in Jesus Christ
    are saying
    now and tomorrow and forever.
           —Ann Weems, *Searching for Shalom*, 55

DAY 4

God of faithfulness,
    how blessed we are to have these stories
    of women of faith;
women who stood by one another
    in joy and in sorrow,
    in sickness and in health.

Ruth, a young woman,
    still with so much life ahead of her;
Naomi, the elder,
    with her whole life behind her.
Although their lives seemed at an end,
    it was only the beginning.

Blood is not always thicker than water.

I want to be like Ruth,
    willing to go to uncharted territory
    trusting, and trusted;
I want to be like Naomi,

setting Ruth free from obligation,
and finding Ruth right back at her side.

Lord God, help us each to know
that home is not so much where we are
but who is there with us.
Help us to know
that home is where you are,
and where you are, is home.

God of faithfulness
let me be a woman of faith.
Amen.

⚬⚬⚬

DAY 5
Riding the Roller Coaster

Some say that the world is divided into two types of people: those who divide people into two types of people and those who don't. I say the world is divided into two types of people: those who love roller coasters and those who don't.

I don't.

Unfortunately my husband and three kids all do. Which leaves me to fend for myself when it comes to amusement parks, unless I ride the kiddie rides, which isn't such a bad thing.

I could blame my dislike of roller coasters on the fact that they make me nauseous and dizzy, two states of being that I don't particularly relish. Yet do I blame my inner ear or my cowardly stomach? Or is it simply the fear of the unknown—the rushing down hills and making sudden twists and turns into uncharted loops and dives—that turns my stomach? That's one question that will just have to remain unanswered.

I don't like the unknown. I like to chart my days, follow

agendas, keep as many loose ends tied as possible. I like to know what each day will bring. I like living in the same area for a long time. I like putting down roots and letting them wend their way deep into the earth, undisturbed.

Which is one reason I admire the biblical Ruth so much. Her life had been turned upside down, her future taken away from her with the death of her husband. Her seemingly predictable life as a wife and potential mother came crashing down and left her with nothing but uncertainty. Returning to her familiar homeland, among relatives who had raised her for the first half of her life and knew her as well as anyone, probably had a great deal of appeal to someone whose future had been swept away by a tidal wave of unfortunate events.

But Ruth didn't take the predictable, safe way out. She chose to stick with her mother-in-law, Naomi, who planned to return to her own homeland in Bethlehem, a place where she hadn't lived in a long, long time; a place where Ruth had never been. Hold your breath! Sharp curve ahead! Roller coaster ride!

I admire those who take a deep breath and grab the rails, maybe emitting a scream or two of fear but willing to take a ride that will lead them to new and unknown places.

For Ruth, that roller coaster took her to wonderful heights: a new husband, a son, a grandson named Jesse, and a great-grandson named David.

Thank goodness for people who aren't afraid to hop on the roller coaster, hang on tight, and even, perhaps, raise their hands in the air and enjoy the ride.

⸺ ᏟᏅ ᏟᏅ ⸺

DAY 6

"Faith is not being sure where you're going, but going anyway. A journey without maps."

—Frederick Buechner, *Beyond Words*, 109

DAY 7

Breath Prayer: Close your eyes; take several slow, deep breaths; then silently pray this breath prayer in rhythm with your breathing. Repeat several times.

*I will follow you
for you are my God.*

— Light your Sabbath Celebration candle. Sit quietly for five minutes.
— Read the Bible passage for this week: Ruth 1:16–17.
— Quietly reflect on the family to whom you belong. What do you know about your ancestors?
— The story of Ruth is one of extreme faithfulness and devotion. What inspires this kind of faithfulness and devotion in you? Who are the people who are devoted to you?
— In your journal, write down some family stories about your ancestors. What helps you to feel connected to the people from your past? If you do not have strong ties to your own family, is there another family to which you feel that you belong? A church family? A neighbor? A friend?
— Thank God for faithfulness and devotion, and for family connections.

The Sabbath comes like a caress, wiping away fear, sorrow and somber memories. (Abraham Joshua Heschel, 68)

WEEK 2

DAY 1

Read the following Bible passage each day this week:
Mark 14:17–19, 29–31.

> When it was evening, [Jesus] came with the twelve.
> And when they had taken their places and were eat-
> ing, Jesus said, "Truly I tell you, one of you will
> betray me, one who is eating with me." They began
> to be distressed and to say to him one after another,
> "Surely, not I?" . . .
>   Peter said to him, "Even though all become
> deserters, I will not." Jesus said to him, "Truly I tell
> you, this day, this very night, before the cock crows
> twice, you will deny me three times." But he said
> vehemently, "Even though I must die with you, I will
> not deny you." And all of them said the same.

Spirit Booster: Reaching In
Jesus invited all of the disciples to the Last Supper, even
though he knew one would betray him. Think about how
Jesus invites you to discipleship, no matter what you have
done with your life.

Spirit Booster: Reaching Out

Is there someone who has betrayed you in some small or large way? Ask God for the strength and faith to try and forgive. Or, if you have betrayed a trust that another has put in you, ask God to help you seek forgiveness.

CRD CRD

DAY 2
Jesus and the Blankie

Our church is gifted with a collection of beautiful banners made by several women from the congregation. We have banners for many seasons of the year. Each Sunday during Lent, for instance, we hang a banner in the chancel, then move it to a side wall the following week when the next banner is hung. Not only are the banners exquisite, they help us mark the passing of time and lend an atmosphere to the worship setting.

One year for Lent, we used the banners as "prompts" for the children's time. Each week in worship, we gathered the children by the banner and then talked about its symbolism and meaning. Week by week, the children (and the adults) listened as either my husband or I talked about the banner. The visual richness, combined with stories or explanations, kept everyone's attention.

The Sunday before Easter, the banner depicted a dark, empty cross with a shroud—a flowing strip of material—wrapped around the crossbars, to remind us of Good Friday, of Jesus on the cross and then wrapped in a shroud in the grave.

I asked the children to examine the banner carefully, then asked them, "What do you see?"

"A cross," a couple of children chimed in. Smart kids.

"And what do you think that is, wrapped around the cross?" I asked next, pointing to the shroud.

One little boy gazed thoughtfully at the banner, his big, brown eyes shining. "I know!" he piped up excitedly. "That's Jesus' blankie!"

I'll bet that most of us, when we were little, had a security blanket, or at the very least, know someone who did — or does. I had one — several, in fact, because I kept wearing them out. My mother, in desperation, cut one of my blankets in half so that she could throw one or the other halves into the wash every now and then and thus keep them somewhat clean.

My brother had two security blankets. One day my mother, thinking that my brother had finally outgrown them, threw the two ratty-looking blankets into the trash. My brother, who had *not* outgrown his need for these unrecognizable hunks of cloth, salvaged his beloved blankets from the trash and hid them where Mom could not find them — between the mattress and box springs of his bed. When Mom saw my brother's bed — with a huge lump like the back of a camel — she realized her error and let him keep the blankets.

The security blanket is a universal symbol in the language of little children. It means just that — security. The "blankie" gives a child something to hang onto in an often frightening world, a sacred, tangible piece of comfort that can go anywhere. Even after we are "too old" to drag our blankies around, we never truly outgrow our need for them.

As the children gathered around the banner in church that Sunday in Lent, an image flashed through my mind: Jesus sitting at the table with his disciples for a final meal, a few hours away from the horror of the cross, death, and denial.

I looked at the little boy with the big, brown eyes. "You know," I said, "I think Jesus might have needed a blankie right about then."

DAY 3
And Then I Heard the Rooster Crow

It was the first day of the Feast, when we ate bread that
   had no yeast
And spent our daylight hours in fast, in honor of our
   sacred past.
Before the closing of the day, as shadows swept the sun
   away,
Our Jesus asked us to prepare an upper room so we
   could share
A meal together on that night, when death would come
   to quench the light.
When evening came, we twelve arrived. We took our
   places by his side.
He sat and watched us while we ate, and then, as if to
   demonstrate,
He took the loaf and held it up, then broke the bread and
   blessed the cup,
And said, "This is my body—take, and eat—I do this for
   your sake.
This cup, my blood poured out for you, to seal God's
   covenant anew."
I watched him in the candle's glow, his eyes were sad, I
   did not know
That soon I'd hear the rooster crow.

We sang a hymn and then went out, and gathered there,
   upon the Mount.
He spoke to us, his voice was hushed, his shoulders
   sagged, his spirit crushed.
He said, "You claim that you believe, yet every one of
   you will leave

On this, the last night of my life." His words cut through
   me like a knife.
We all exclaimed with one accord, "We never will desert
   you, Lord!"
And I spoke louder than the rest: "My love for you shall
   stand the test,
For even if the others flee, you always can depend on
   me!"
Then Jesus heaved a weary sigh, and turned, and looked
   me in the eye.
"Dear Peter, can you truly say that you alone have found
   the way?
Your spirit's keen, but flesh is weak. You will betray the
   One you seek.
Three times tonight, you will forego all ties with me. It
   shall be so,
Before you hear the rooster crow."

I had no words to answer him. And as the evening stars
   grew dim,
We left the mount and went to pray. I still denied that I'd
   betray
This man I'd follow anywhere, whose heart was filled
   with such despair.
We came upon a quiet place. He knelt in prayer, and
   bowed his face,
And asked if we would watch and wait. But we were
   tired, and it was late.
So while he prayed, we fell asleep. We left him there,
   alone, to weep.
Then with some others, Judas came and kissed our Lord,
   and called his name.
With bitter rage, with clubs and sword, the angry mob,
   they took our Lord
And dragged him off before our eyes; but none of us
   would compromise

Our safety. No! We turned and ran, all twelve of us, his
    faithless clan.

I hid myself, and felt such woe. I knew that I had failed
    him, though
I had not heard the rooster crow.

I followed at a distance, then, to see just how it all would
    end.
A crowd had gathered in the yard. I found a place among
    the guard.
Though chilled, I felt myself perspire, and pushed my
    way up to the fire.
But though my hands and face grew hot, my feet were
    frozen to the spot.
A slave-girl came upon the scene: "This man was with
    the Nazarene!"
"Not me!" I cried. "You must be wrong! I do not to that
    man belong!"
And then I heard it, soft and low:
The first cry of the rooster's crow.

The slave-girl said to me again, "I know that you are one
    of them!"
And I denied it, louder still; my body shook, my voice
    was shrill.
A third time, someone said to me, "You're with the man
    from Galilee!"
I panicked with the fearful thought that just like Jesus,
    I'd been caught.
So one last time, I shouted, "No! I do not know him! Let
    me go!"
And then, I heard the rooster crow.

I fell upon my face, and sobbed, surrounded by the
    hostile mob.

My soul was filled with bitter tears. I was no stronger
than my fears.
He chose me, Peter, from his flock, and told me I would
be the rock
On which his kingdom would be built. That rock had
crumbled into silt.
I thought my faith was so mature. I was so brave! Now
I'm not sure.
I wish that I had spoken out, instead of being ruled by
doubt.
You think, if you'd been there with me, that you'd have
done things differently?
Then think again! And count the times that you've
engaged in equal crimes.
How often do you turn in shame when someone
mentions Jesus' name?
Or fail to speak up when you see some act of cruel
brutality?

So silently the wind does blow, but listen close — as
shadows grow,
And you may hear the rooster crow.
Yes, you will hear the rooster crow.

It was the first day of the Feast . . .

DAY 4

Help us, O God, to find here tonight,
Wisdom to know what is right,
And strength to do what is right.
Enlighten our minds with your truth;
Warm our hearts with your love;
Fill our lives with your power,

That we may go out to live for you: through Jesus
Christ our Lord. Amen.
—William Barclay, *A Barclay Prayer Book*, 184

DAY 5
Broken for You

So much of Jesus' ministry centered around a meal.

After his temptation in the wilderness, angels brought
him food and drink and then "waited on him" (Matthew
4:11), perhaps with a fine cloth draped over an angelic
arm as wine was poured.

His first miracle occurred at a wedding, amid much
feasting and, yes, drinking of wine.

He ate with Pharisees and those others considered "sin-
ners," with Mary and Martha and multitudes of strangers.
He picnicked with thousands, plucked grain on the Sabbath, and got in trouble for doing so. And as a last act of
friendship and Saviorship, he broke bread with his disciples on the final night of his earthly life.

How he ate that last meal, knowing that one of the
eleven seated around that table with him was about to turn
him in, is truly amazing. Did the bread stick in his throat?
Did he have to choke down the wine? It's hard to eat when
death hovers by your shoulder like a nervous waiter.

But Jesus broke the bread and poured the wine, and
said, "Take, eat, drink: this is my body, broken for you."

Broken for you. For you, Peter, who sank in the water
like a stone, who will deny me before the night is over.

Broken for you. For you, James and John, though you
bicker like the brothers that you are, arguing over who is
best and most deserves a seat of honor.

Broken for you. For you, Matthew, tax collector, out-
cast of society.

Broken for you. For you, Judas, although I know full well what you are about to do.

This is what Christ does for us. He sits at the table and breaks the bread and makes sure everyone, *everyone*, is fed, even when the meal sits like a large lump of wax in his own stomach.

"Truly I tell you, one of you will betray me, one who is eating with me," Jesus says on that last night (Mark 14:18). And all those gathered are aghast. "Surely not I?"

Yes, surely you. You and you and you. You and I, we all do, in our own way. We all betray the one who breaks the bread of life and lets his body be broken for us anyway.

DAY 6

"An unbelieved truth can hurt a man much more than a lie. It takes great courage to back truth unacceptable to our times. There's a punishment for it, and it's usually crucifixion. I haven't the courage for that."

—John Steinbeck, *East of Eden*, 303

DAY 7

Breath Prayer: Close your eyes; take several slow, deep breaths; then silently pray this breath prayer in rhythm with your breathing. Repeat several times.

*Jesus, I thank you
for my place at your table.*

— Light your Sabbath Celebration candle. Sit quietly for five minutes.

— Read the Bible passage for this week: Mark 14:17–19, 29–31.
— Quietly reflect on the Last Supper: the disciples gathered around the table, eating and talking, and Jesus knowing that one of them would betray him.
— How do you think the mood around the table changed when Jesus made his announcement? If you had been one of the disciples with Jesus that night, what would your reaction have been?
— In your journal, write down the ways in which you have felt betrayed and how that felt or still feels. Then write down the times when you have been the one to break a trust, and how that felt or still feels.
— Pray to forgive those who have broken your trust; and ask forgiveness for the trusts you have broken and the times you have denied your faith in Jesus.

"And forgive us our sins,
  for we ourselves forgive everyone indebted to us." (Luke 11:4)

WEEK 3

DAY 1

Read the following Bible passage each day this week: Psalm 1:1–2.

> Happy are those
>> who do not follow the advice of the wicked,
> or take the path that sinners tread,
>> or sit in the seat of scoffers;
> but their delight is in the law of the LORD,
>> and on his law they meditate day and night.

Spirit Booster: Reaching In
What are your favorite Bible verses? Write down a few of them on different index cards and place them in places where you will find them later: in a coat pocket, a drawer, a purse, a closet. You'll have fun finding these when you aren't even looking for them!

Spirit Booster: Reaching Out
Donate a new or gently used Bible to an organization that serves the homeless, abused women, or underprivileged children.

DAY 2
Living the Dash

I'm not bothered by walking through cemeteries. Perhaps it comes from growing up near a cemetery, and then from being a pastor and spending a lot of time at cemeteries. I find it peaceful to walk among the graves. I am deeply fascinated by the names on the headstones and the different markers and memorials, and by imagining the lives of the people who are buried there. Many gravestones are so old that the letters have been completely worn off. Some of the gravestones are huge, massive slabs of marble or granite. Others are very modest and hardly noticeable. I saw a gravestone once with a bowling pin and bowling ball etched next to the name.

Whatever the size, shape, or age of gravestones, almost all have one mark in common: the little dash symbol between the dates of a person's birth and death. Sometimes the death date isn't yet etched in stone, but the dash is there, ready to connect the beginning and the end of that person's life. The one exception is when a baby is born and dies on the same day. Seeing that on a gravestone, you cannot help but ache for the life that never even got to have its own little dash.

Our life is that dash—that little punctuation mark between our birth and our death. Everything that happens to us happens in that dash. None of us knows how many years our dash will represent until it's all over. We might have ten years; we might have a hundred. What will that dash mean when your life is over, when both dates have been etched on your gravestone?

"As you therefore have received Christ Jesus the Lord, continue to live your lives in him, rooted and built up in him and established in the faith, just as you were taught, abounding in thanksgiving," Paul writes (Colossians 2:6–7). Good advice no matter what each day brings. We cannot predict how our lives will turn out, and we don't always have a choice in the situations that will fill out the dash. No matter how good or bad or in-between each day is, we can choose to live as people of faith, watering and nourishing our souls so that our roots of faith grow deep and sure, and so that others will know us to be people of thanksgiving.

We fill in the dash between the date of our birth and the date of our death more by how we choose to live what happens rather than simply by what happens. In the end, it isn't going to matter if you lived some grand and glorious life, or if you left a huge mark on the world, or if you were the absolute "greatest" athlete or businessperson or politician.

One day, your life will be finished. It may be just a short sprint. It may end up a marathon. What counts is not the number of years you have; it's how you fill in the dash.

DAY 3

You are blessed
when you spend time with God,
and with God's word.
When you do,
then you won't be
so likely to depend on the advice
of people who may not have
your best interests in mind.

When you spend time with God,
and with God's word,
you won't feel as though you have to
go along with the crowd when the crowd isn't making
very good choices. For instance:
the people who make fun
of God, or who ridicule those

who have faith, so that you feel strange admitting
that you believe in God or go
to church or that faith is an important part
of who you are.

Instead, why not be the person who delights
in learning about God and God's
ways? You will be much more
likely to keep in a good frame
of mind, to find joy in
each day, and to know that you
are blessed. Immersing yourself in God's
word, and living your faith
each day makes you feel
alive!

You will be refreshed!
Like drinking a cup of ice-cold
water on a hot and humid day.

Drink up God's word as you do
that cup of water. Oh, how good
that water tastes! Oh, how God's word
fills you to the brim! Your thirst
will be quenched.

And even when there is war
and terrorism and violence; even
when you yourself are going through
rough times, or feel frustrated, frightened,
or flustered; you know that you will
find your way, because God is with
you, every moment. That's what God
promises. And that is what you will discover
for yourself when you keep company with
God every day.

DAY 4
Deliver us from amnesia

God of peace,
God of justice,
God of freedom,
    We give you thanks for your cadences of
        peace, justice, and freedom,
    Cadences that have surged through the lives
        of Martin,
        and Ralph,
        and Rosa,
        and John,
        and Fred,
        and Hosea,
        and Jesse,
        and Andy,
and all that nameless mass of risk-takers who have been
    obedient to your promises
    and susceptible to your dreams.
Deliver us from amnesia
    concerning their courage in the face of violence,
        their peace-making against hate,
        and their hunger for you in a devouring economy.
Deliver us from amnesia:
        turn our memory into hope,
        turn our gratitude into energy,
        turn our well-being into impatience.
That these same cadences of your will may pulse even
    among us.
Amen.

—Walter Brueggemann, *Awed to Heaven,*
Rooted in Earth, 103

DAY 5
Happy Are Those

In the church I serve, we give Bibles to children when they reach second grade. At that point, the children have graduated from our Children in Worship program that coincides with worship (no, we do not have Sunday school and worship at the same time!) and now find themselves in the sanctuary for the full hour of worship (and, yes, we do try to keep worship to an hour). We encourage parents and children to follow along in their Bibles when we read the Scripture lesson for the day. It's quite a wonderful sight to look out over the sanctuary and see adults and children with their heads bowed over Bibles, their fingers tracing the words as we read from the pulpit. It sure beats looking out and seeing people with their heads bowed and bobbing as they drift off for a short nap!

We make a big deal out of handing out the Bibles. We call the children forward to stand in front of the congregation, then call each one by name as we hand them their freshly personalized copy of God's word. The younger brothers and sisters aren't so fond of this, as they zealously—or is that jealously?—watch.

The best part is that the children see the receiving of a Bible as a precious gift. Their faces light up, they stand up straight as they can, and as soon as the Bibles are all handed out, they eagerly flip through the pages, oblivious to the rest of the folks around them. Many of the adults comment afterwards on how wonderful it was to see the children glowing with the joy of receiving God's holy word.

Would that we all looked at our Bibles that way: eager to flip them open and pour over the pages, delighted with the joy of being handed such a precious gift.

DAY 6

"It is a mistake to look to the Bible to close a discussion; the Bible seeks to open one."

—William Sloane Coffin, *Credo*, 145

DAY 7

Breath Prayer: Close your eyes; take several slow, deep breaths; then silently pray this breath prayer in rhythm with your breathing. Repeat several times.

*My delight, O Lord,
is in your law.*

— Light your Sabbath Celebration candle. Sit quietly for five minutes.
— Read the Bible passage for this week: Psalm 1:1–2.
— Quietly reflect on the gift of God's word. What do you remember about your first Bible? How old were you when you received it? Do you have a family Bible that has been passed down to you?
— There are many places in the world where reading the Bible is illegal and puts a person's life at risk. How blessed we are to read the Bible without such constraints! Reflect on the great privilege we have to read the Bible freely.
— In your journal, write down your memories of your first Bible, or a Bible that you have that is of particular importance to you and explain why.
— Thank God for the gift of the word and the Word.

Your decrees are wonderful;
   therefore my soul keeps them.
The unfolding of your words gives light.
(Psalm 119:129–130)

WEEK 4

DAY 1

Read the following Bible passage each day this week: Colossians 2:6–7.

> As you therefore have received Christ Jesus the Lord, continue to live your lives in him, rooted and built up in him and established in the faith, just as you were taught, abounding in thanksgiving.

Spirit Booster: Reaching In
Remember as a child what fun it was to wrap a bean seed in a wet paper towel and then place it in a clear plastic bag and watch the roots and plant start to grow? Try this experiment again, thinking this time about how your life is rooted in Christ.

Spirit Booster: Reaching Out
Give a small plant to a friend or a neighbor, with a note attached: "Thank you for helping me find my roots in Christ."

DAY 2
Rooting for Roots

Transplanting a tree is a lot different from moving a flower from one spot in the garden to another. There's this thing about trees called "root balls."

Root balls tend to be quite large. The roots of a newly planted tree grow rapidly from fall through spring, especially in areas where trees lose their leaves in the fall and re-leaf in warmer weather. Once spring arrives, the tree's efforts turn to the top growth: buds and leaves, flowers and fruit. The root ball has to be established when the top growth is at a minimum.

A healthy tree has a very large root ball. When moving the tree, the new hole has to be shallow, yet three times the diameter of the root ball. This can translate into a very large hole! But it is important that the tree have healthy, strong roots; that they be given the room they need to grow; and that they be planted close enough to the surface to get the oxygen they need to take root in the new surroundings.

A tree without a healthy root ball probably will not survive being transplanted. Even with a healthy root ball and a properly dug hole, some trees don't hold up very well, literally and figuratively. With strong roots, the tree has a far better chance not only of surviving but of thriving.

In Paul's letter to the Colossian church, he encourages the new Christians to establish their roots in Christ so that they can build upon their faith in the years to come. The roots of faith are essential in the present time but are necessary for the future as well. Without a faith founded in Christ, the changes and "transplantings" that come about in life have the capacity to uproot us and leave us floundering. Strong roots of faith only grow when they are carefully tended to, watered and fed and nurtured and given oxygen to breathe and light for life.

Even with a strongly rooted faith, we can find ourselves beaten down by storms, shriveling when the heat gets too high, or struggling just to hold fast.

A tree carefully planted grows into a magnificent, strong creation that provides shelter and shade, beauty and bounty. At that point, the roots aren't even always visible, but they're there, growing deeper all the time.

DAY 3
Relapse

Out of the wound we pluck
The shrapnel. Thorns we squeeze
Out of the hand. Even poison forth we suck,
And after pain have ease.

But images that grow
Within the soul have life
Like cancer and, often cut, live on below
The deepest of the knife,

Waiting their time to shoot
At some defenceless hour
Their poison, unimpaired, at the heart's root,
And, like a golden shower,

Unanswerably sweet,
Bright with returning guilt,
Fatally in a moment's time defeat
Our brazen towers long-built;

And all our former pain
And all our surgeon's care
Is lost, and all the unbearable (in vain
Borne once) is still to bear.
—C. S. Lewis, *Poems*, 103–104

DAY 4

You are holy, Lord, the only God,
    and your deeds are wonderful.
You are love, you are wisdom.
You are humility, you are endurance.
You are rest, you are peace.
You are joy and gladness.
You are all our riches, and you suffice for us.
You are beauty, you are gentleness.
You are our protector,
You are our guardian and defender.
You are courage,
You are our haven and hope,
You are our faith, our great consolation.
You are our eternal life, great and wonderful Lord,
God almighty, merciful Saviour.

—St. Francis of Assisi, *The Book of a Thousand Prayers*, 78

∞∞

DAY 5
Plant Food

It's fun to get metaphorical about being "rooted in Christ," to compare it to plants and trees and flowers and such needing strong roots if they are to grow and flourish.

But what exactly does it mean, to be rooted in Christ?

I spent a good deal of time puzzling over this. I thought about using metaphors such as "we water the roots of faith by reading the Bible," which is true enough but also somewhat trite.

So, I read and reread the Scripture passage for this week: "As you therefore have received Christ Jesus the

Lord, continue to live your lives in him, rooted and built up in him and established in the faith, just as you were taught, abounding in thanksgiving" (Colossians 2:6–7). I walked around the house, got a drink of water, brushed my teeth, came back and read and reread the passage again.

Then it struck me: the answer was right there in the passage!

What does it mean to be rooted in Christ? It means that we are *thankful*; and not just thankful, but *abounding* in thanksgiving! We are grateful—joyfully so—for the amazing grace God offers to us in Jesus Christ.

Do you believe in Jesus Christ? Be thankful!

Do you take time to read the Bible? Be thankful!

Do you pray? Be thankful!

Are you part of a community of faith? Be thankful!

Imagine how disappointing it must be to Jesus when our faith becomes dreary, depressing, or dutiful. It's like your child saying, "I love you, Mom," without one iota of truth or enthusiasm. Who wants to hear that?

A faith rooted in Christ—rooted in thankfulness for Christ—is a faith that abounds in joy and gratitude, a faith that makes others want to find that kind of faith as well.

Practice being thankful for Christ, even if it's just saying, simply, "Thank you, God, for Jesus Christ." Beginning and ending each day with those words might just be the framework needed for a strong, vital, and, yes, *rooted* faith.

Thanks be to God!

DAY 6

"Loyalty is so fierce and contagious an energy that it is safe only when the object of it is something that we can love or worship when we are alone."
—William L. Sullivan, *The Westminster Collection of Christian Quotations*, 239

DAY 7

Breath Prayer: Close your eyes; take several slow, deep breaths; then silently pray this breath prayer in rhythm with your breathing. Repeat several times.

*My life is rooted
in you, O Christ.*

— Light your Sabbath Celebration candle. Sit quietly for five minutes.
— Read the Bible passage for this week: Colossians 2:6–7.
— Quietly reflect on the image of being rooted in Christ. What holds your "faith roots" in place?
— Do you remember your baptism? Or do you remember the story because of what you have been told by your family and those who were present? What do you know about when you received this sacrament? What does it mean in your life that you have been baptized in Christ Jesus? (If you are not baptized, would you like to be? What has kept that from happening in your life?)
— In your journal, write down ways you plan to "continue to live your life in Christ," as Scripture tells us to do.
— Pray that your life will always be rooted in Christ and that those roots will be strong and able to withstand the challenges of life.

Labor is a craft, but perfect rest is an art. It is the result of an accord of body, mind, and imagination. (Abraham Joshua Heschel, 14)

AUGUST
BLESSING

WEEK 1

DAY 1

Read the following Bible passage each day this week: Numbers 6:24–26.

> The LORD bless you and keep you;
> the LORD make his face to shine upon you,
>   and be gracious to you;
> the LORD lift up his countenance upon you,
>   and give you peace.

Spirit Booster: Reaching In
Close your eyes, and feel the warmth of God's face shining upon you like soft sunlight.

Spirit Booster: Reaching Out
The next time you are out in a crowd or gathering of people, imagine God's face shining softly upon theirs. You may end up seeing people in a different "light."

DAY 2
Words of Blessing

Every time I give the benediction at the close of worship, I use these words from Numbers:

> The LORD bless you and keep you;
> the LORD make his face to shine upon you,
>   and be gracious to you;
> the LORD lift up his countenance upon you,
>   and give you peace.

I've said it often enough that I have the words down pat. I time my delivery so that I scan the entire congregation as well as the choir behind me. Yet I am intentional about not just scanning the congregation but also trying to look as many people as possible right in the eye, which is a big task in a church that regularly seats about 150 to 200 people each service. That's a lot of eyes!

But it seems to me that the words are much more powerful if I can actually look directly into someone's eyes, rather than send the blessing skimming across the tops of the people's heads.

I look in the eyes of the woman who recently lost her husband as I utter the words "bless you."

I look in the eyes of the older gentleman who is contemplating a move to a long-term care facility as I say the words "and keep you."

I look in the eyes of the teenager who feels wrapped in darkness as I say the words "shine upon you."

I look in the eyes of the newly divorced young mother as I say "be gracious to you."

I look in the eyes of the fellow who recently lost his job as I say the words "lift up."

I look in the eyes of the couple struggling to have a child as I say the words "give you peace."

It doesn't always turn out so exact, but no matter what, I try to look people in the eyes when I offer the blessing.

After a few years of using this same benediction over and over, I thought about changing it. That Sunday, as I pronounced the words of blessing, as I looked people in the eye, I noticed that, throughout the sanctuary, a strange thing was happening.

People were silently mouthing the words along with me.

It took me by surprise—but what a delight!

These words from an ancient text, spoken first back in the time of Moses, were words that were bringing comfort each week to the people of my congregation. Wow.

I hope that the words have become so ingrained that during the week when a particular person is in need of a blessing, he or she will be able to mouth the words in a silent and yet oh-so-powerful benediction of praise and hope.

DAY 3
Eternal Yes!

O God, you bless
with such excess
I can't find words that will express
my happiness.

In my distress
when I confess
you graciously clean up my mess.
Success!

Don't have to guess
I can express
my trust in all your faithfulness
Eternal *YES!*

DAY 4

In me there is darkness,
But with you there is light;
I am lonely, but you do not leave me;
I am feeble in heart, but with you there is help;
I am restless, but with you there is peace.
In me there is bitterness, but with you there is patience;
I do not understand your ways,
But you know the way for me.
  — Dietrich Bonhoeffer, *The One Year Book of Personal*
Prayer, March 26

DAY 5
Let's Face It

What is the difference between a "face" and a "countenance"?

After twenty years of pronouncing the benediction from the Old Testament book of Numbers ("the Lord make his face to shine upon you . . . the Lord lift up his countenance upon you . . .") I decided it was time to find out.

I asked my friend, Phil, a member of my congregation and a scholar who actually reads from the Greek Bible — in the Greek — and who knows Latin and some Hebrew as well. He asked his brother, who taught himself to read

Hebrew (okay, now I'm really feeling humbled!). The answer made me wish I'd asked the question a long time ago, but it's never too late to learn.

As in most languages, words can have multiple meanings, and in the Hebrew, words have multiple meanings in multiple contexts. The Hebrew word used in the passage from Numbers, *panav*, comes from the root word, *panim*, which means "face." The same word is used in the Hebrew text of Numbers for what we have translated as "face" and "countenance." Thus, the English translation for *panav* includes the metaphorical meaning of "face" as well as the literal meaning.

To "make one's face shine" can also be translated as "deal kindly with you" or "make one's presence enlighten you." "Lifting up" one's face means to "bestow favor." In the Jewish tradition, God does not have physical attributes, so all these are understood in the sense of "Lordship," "Kingship," or "Guardianship."

Imagine, then, entering the presence of the Lord. How will this all-powerful, all-knowing Lord react to you? I think of the scene in the movie *The Wizard of Oz*, when the trembling Dorothy and her misfit companions come to see the Great Oz. They bow down, scared out of their wits, and the Great Oz (or his fake persona) flares up in a burst of flame accompanied by ominous sounds, and that huge, mean face scowls unmercifully upon them. Let's face it: Who wants to be in the presence of someone who responds to you like that?

Not so the Lord. The Lord sees you—actually turns, faces you, and smiles at you—and by so doing blesses you. And your insides, all tight and nervous and terrified, relax, and the ice melts, and you feel the warmth, the shine, of the Lord's gracious love and blessing. Wow.

At the start of every Sabbath, Jewish parents recite this blessing to their children. What a beautiful and marvelous way to enter into a time of holiness and worship!

Maybe the phrases from Numbers should be recited as a call to worship, and not just a benediction. Still, it doesn't hurt to be sent out into an often cold and cruel world with the light of God's countenance shining upon us for all the world to see.

Face it: Either way, you can't go wrong.

DAY 6

"In the biblical sense, if you give me your blessing, you irreversibly convey into my life not just something of the beneficent power and vitality of who you are, but something also of the life-giving power of God, in whose name the blessing is given."

—Frederick Buechner, *Beyond Words*, 48

DAY 7

Breath Prayer: Close your eyes; take several slow, deep breaths; then silently pray this breath prayer in rhythm with your breathing. Repeat several times.

*Shine your face upon me
and give me peace.*

— Light your Sabbath Celebration candle. Sit quietly for five minutes.
— Read the Bible passage for this week: Numbers 6:24–26.
— Quietly reflect on the sense of peace that is achieved just by reading the words of this Bible passage. Jesus is

the light of the world—and that light shines on you each and every day.

— This Bible passage is often used as a benediction, a closing of worship. It can also be used as a way to start the day. Each day this week, begin your day with this blessing, and end it with this benediction.

— In your journal, write down random words that come to mind when you think of "shine," "peace," and "grace."

— Pray a prayer of thanks for the joy it is to feel the light of God's face shining on you!

To observe the Sabbath is to celebrate the coronation of a day in the spiritual wonderland of time. (Abraham Joshua Heschel, 18)

WEEK 2

DAY 1

Read the following Bible passage each day this week:
Matthew 5:1–12.

> When Jesus saw the crowds, he went up the mountain; and after he sat down, his disciples came to him. Then he began to speak, and taught them, saying:
> "Blessed are the poor in spirit, for theirs is the kingdom of heaven.
> "Blessed are those who mourn, for they will be comforted.
> "Blessed are the meek, for they will inherit the earth.
> "Blessed are those who hunger and thirst for righteousness, for they will be filled.
> "Blessed are the merciful, for they will receive mercy.
> "Blessed are the pure in heart, for they will see God.
> "Blessed are the peacemakers, for they will be called children of God.
> "Blessed are those who are persecuted for righteousness' sake, for theirs is the kingdom of heaven.

"Blessed are you when people revile you and persecute you and utter all kinds of evil against you falsely on my account. Rejoice and be glad, for your reward is great in heaven, for in the same way they persecuted the prophets who were before you."

Spirit Booster: Reaching In
On a notecard, write the words, "Blessed am I when . . . ," and then record the blessings that happen to you each day this week.

Spirit Booster: Reaching Out
Jesus sat down and waited for his disciples to sit down and listen to him. Be aware of how well you listen to others. Give the person talking to you your full attention, whether in person or on the phone, and by so doing you will let that person know how important it is for you to listen to him or her.

DAY 2
First Person Sermon

Try to imagine what the crowds must have thought, clustered on the grassy hillside, the sun warming their faces while hope warms their souls. They've come to hear this Jesus, this prophet, teacher, healer; they've come to hear some words, words that will lift them up and not let them down.

Jesus begins to speak: "Blessed are the poor in spirit, for theirs is the kingdom of heaven." The words hang in the stillness like pregnant rain clouds, heavy and ripe.

Jesus goes on, listing blessings one by one. They are music to the people's ears, no doubt, although as he continues, it is clear that Jesus isn't just trying to make people feel good. Following the blessings are words that demand responsibility, service, and risk.

In Matthew's Gospel, the verses in chapters 5–7 constitute Jesus' first public sermon, his first major address to the crowds who have begun to buzz about this newcomer in their midst. Wise men have followed the star to greet him after his birth, John the Baptist dunks him in the river Jordan, and the devil tries to get him to turn stones into bread. But the only words that Jesus has spoken, aside from putting the devil in place, are to a few scattered folks that he invites to come, follow him.

What powerful words for a first sermon. What an out-of-this-world and yet very much in-this-world message to convey to the crowds.

The words of blessing and what follow set the tone for all of Jesus' ministry. Be a follower of me, Jesus says, and you will be blessed. Be a follower of me, and you will learn a way of life that is different from what the world deems important. Be a follower of me, and I will lead you. Be a follower of me, and you will put your life on the line.

What a magnificent preacher! Words of grace, words of challenge, and words of truth, all wrapped up in that one sermon.

And if anyone ever practiced what he or she preached . . .

DAY 3

There's also this to see: They will live on, they will
    increase,
no longer pawns of time.
They will grow like the sweet wild berries
the forest ripens as its treasure.

Then blessed are those who never turned away

and blessed are those who stood quietly in the rain.
Theirs shall be the harvest; for them the fruits.

They will outlast the pomp and power
of lawmakers, whose meanings will crumble.
When all else is exhausted and bled of purpose,
they will lift their hands, that have survived.
— Rainer Maria Rilke, *Rilke's Book of Hours*, 143–45

DAY 4

O God, our Father,
Bless our friends and our loved ones and keep them safe
from harm and danger.
Bless our enemies and those who dislike us, and help us
by caring for them to make them our friends.
Bless those who are in pain of body, anxiety of mind, and
sorrow of heart.
Bless those who are lonely because death has taken a
dear one from them.
Bless those who are old and who now are left alone.
Bless those who have made a mess of life and who know
well that they have no one but themselves to blame.
Bless those who have fallen to temptation and who are
sorry now, and give them grace to begin again and
this time not to fall.
Bless all who are in trouble and help them to win their
way through it.
Bless each one of us as you know we need.
Amen.
— William Barclay, *A Barclay Prayer Book*, 192–93

DAY 5
When the Words Hit Home

I remember the first time I preached on the Beatitudes: February 1, 1987.

I don't have that great of a memory, and probably couldn't name the dates of any other sermons I've preached over the last twenty years (save Christmas Eve).

But I will always remember the date of February 1, because when I returned home from worship that afternoon I received the phone call telling me that my dear Aunt Arlene had died of cancer at the age of forty-seven.

The words of the Beatitudes really hit home for me that day, especially the ones about "blessed are the pure in heart, for they will see God," because Arlene had a clear and pure heart; and "blessed are those who mourn, for they will be comforted," because I was certainly in need of comfort right then. I mourned because I loved Arlene, always felt a special connection with her. I mourned because I was seven months pregnant with our second child, and now Arlene would never meet her. I grieved for my grandmother who was about to bury the second of five adult children (she would bury another before too many years). Grief descended upon our family, and we needed comfort right then and there. Surely, we would need comfort later as well, but the promise of immediate comfort was what meant the most.

Jesus doesn't say, "Blessed you will be, many years from now." The words of the Beatitudes speak of immediate blessing, in all kinds of circumstances, for all kinds of people who are most in need of a word of good news and comfort.

As I hung up the phone that morning, I knew that I was going to have to practice what I had just preached, to believe the good news in a deeper way than I had before. With the words of Jesus still ringing in my ears and vibrating in my heart, I prayed a silent word of thanks to God.

DAY 6

"The stumbling block for most sensitive nonbelievers is not Christ but Christians, not God but suffering and the fact that the church in its hour of prosperity has worked so little for its alleviation."

—William Sloane Coffin, *Credo,* 144

DAY 7

Breath Prayer: Close your eyes; take several slow, deep breaths; then silently pray this breath prayer in rhythm with your breathing. Repeat several times.

Jesus, I come to you,
seeking your blessing.

— Light your Sabbath Celebration candle. Sit quietly for five minutes.
— Read the Bible passage for this week: Matthew 5:1–12.
— Quietly reflect on the scene in Matthew. Jesus sees the large crowds. He walks up the mountain so he can see and be seen by the people. He sits down and waits. His disciples come to him. Then he speaks. Do you imagine the crowd to be quiet, straining to hear every word? Do you see yourself in the crowd, looking up the mountain

towards Jesus, or as one of the disciples sitting at his feet?

— With which of these blessings do you most identify? Why is that? Where are you seeking blessing in your life?

— In your journal, be as specific as you can in identifying your place within this Bible passage. Are you feeling poor in spirit? Are you in mourning? Are you a peace-maker? Do you feel blessed in these times?

— Pray for God to bless you, that you might be a blessing to others.

The Sabbath teaches all beings whom to praise. (Abraham Joshua Heschel, 24)

WEEK 3

DAY 1

Read the following Bible passage each day this week:
Psalm 103:1–5.

> Bless the LORD, O my soul,
>   and all that is within me, bless his holy name.
> Bless the LORD, O my soul,
>   and do not forget all his benefits—
> who forgives all your iniquity,
>   who heals all your diseases,
> who redeems your life from the Pit,
>   who crowns you with steadfast love and mercy,
> who satisfies you with good as long as you live
>   so that your youth is renewed like the eagle's.

Spirit Booster: Reaching In
Hold your head high! You are wearing a crown of love
and mercy. Think of this at times when you need a boost.

Spirit Booster: Reaching Out
If you don't have one already, put up an outdoor bird feeder
and know that you are helping to bless God's creation.

DAY 2
Let All That Is within Me

Greg and I were not quite two years into our first parish call when we discovered that we were going to be parents. Of course, we were thrilled. But how to tell the congregation?

The choir took care of that for us. At the annual ice-cream social held on the church lawn on a bright, sunny Sunday afternoon, a trio sang a song from *The Sound of Music*, the one that goes, "Soon the duet will become a trio. . . ." A couple of them knew our secret, and we didn't mind them spreading our good news.

As we laughed and greeted people and ate delicious, homemade ice-cream, one of the elders came up to me. "I had already guessed," he said, "because of your Call to Worship this morning."

My Call to Worship? What in the world had I said?

He saw the puzzled look on my face. "Well," he continued, "there was something about the way you read the words of the Psalm today. 'Bless the Lord, O my soul, *let all that is within me* bless his holy name.' "

Yes, this is a true story! Which goes to show that there were some very perceptive elders in that church, or that a "poker face" is something I simply don't possess.

Let all that is within me bless God. I felt blessed, carrying our first child (and the next two, as well). Even in those early stages, I hoped that our child(ren) would grow up in the faith, to live and breathe and praise the Lord, to bless God's holy name one day when they had the words to do so.

That was twenty years ago, from the time I am writing this. But every time I hear the words of Psalm 103, I can't help but smile and remember that elder, that day, that glorious time in my life.

Let all that is within me bless God's holy name. Indeed.

DAY 3
Jesu

Jesu is in my heart, his sacred name
Is deeply carved there: but the other week
A great affliction broke the little frame
Even all to pieces, which I went to seek:
And first I found the corner where was *J*,
After where *ES* and next where *U* was graved.
When I had got these parcels, instantly
I sat me down to spell them, and perceived
That to my broken heart he was *I ease you,*
And to my whole is *JESU*.
> —George Herbert, *Eerdman's Book of*
> *Christian Poetry*, 29

DAY 4

How can I tell of such love to me?
You made me in your image
   and hold me in the palm of your hand,
   your cords of love, strong and fragile as silk
   bind me and hold me.
Rich cords, to family and friends,
   music and laughter echoing in memories,
   light dancing on the water, hills rejoicing.
Cords that found me hiding behind carefully built walls
     and let me out,
   love that heard my heart break and despair and
     rescued me,
   love that overcame my fears and doubts and released me.
The questions and burdens I carry you take,

to leave my hands free—to hold yours, and others,
free to follow your cords as they move and swirl in the
  breeze,
free to be caught up in the dance of your love,
finding myself in surrendering to you.
How can I tell of such love? How can I give to such love?
I am, here am I.
  —Catherine Hooper, *The Book of a Thousand Prayers*, 75

DAY 5
Star-Spangled Prayer

A kindergartner came home one day with a tape of songs to learn for the kindergarten music concert that would be taking place at school in a few weeks. Wherever she didn't quite know the words, she filled in her own, singing loudly and joyfully, as she danced around the house.

When the music to "The Star-Spangled Banner" started playing, her mother felt some concern. It wasn't her fear that her little girl wouldn't understand words like "perilous" and "ramparts." The mother didn't feel so comfortable with this sweet, innocent child singing about rockets glaring and bombs bursting, even if the song does happen to be our national anthem.

The child plowed through the song, still spinning happily. When she got to the part about "bombs bursting in air," the words were not about bombs at all. The little girl heard—and sang—words with quite another meaning: "and we're twirling in prayer . . ."

Twirling in prayer! What a perfect image for how God wants us to live our lives. Not dropping bombs, even though it can be argued that there are times when this is appropriate. Twirling in prayer might be a better approach to the sorrows of the world, and without a doubt would portray a much more positive image about our role in dealing with the difficult issues of the world.

When I hear the words of Psalm 103, my spirit leaps with joy. How can anyone hear these words without feeling some sense of the delight and gratitude the writer must have felt? Truly, when we are aligned with God's purposes, there can be no other response than joy. Twirling in prayer? That sounds like a great way to express what this psalm is all about.

I'm not sure my congregation would appreciate it if I started spinning around the chancel some Sunday during our time of prayer. We do have liturgical dancers who could do that, but not me. Praying at home when nobody is around to see me? Ah, who knows? You just might catch me twirling in prayer one of these days.

DAY 6

Blessed are those who trust in the LORD,
    whose trust is in the LORD.
They shall be like a tree planted by water,
    sending out its roots by the stream.
                —Jeremiah 17:7–8

DAY 7

Breath Prayer: Close your eyes; take several slow, deep breaths; then silently pray this breath prayer in rhythm with your breathing. Repeat several times.

Bless the Lord, O my soul;
bless God's holy name.

— Light your Sabbath Celebration candle. Sit quietly for five minutes.
— Read the Bible passage for this week: Psalm 103:1–5.
— Quietly reflect on all that God does for you: forgives you, heals you, redeems you, crowns you with love and mercy, satisfies you with good, renews your strength.
— Do you feel satisfied with the way you understand and experience the love of God? What happens in those times when you feel empty or distant from God? How do you find your way back?
— In your journal, write down the Bible reading and replace the pronouns "your" and "you" with "my" and "me."
— Pray for your spiritual strength to be renewed and to be filled with God's goodness.

The seventh day itself is uttering praise. (Abraham Joshua Heschel, 24)

WEEK 4

DAY 1

Read the following Bible passage each day this week: James 1:22–25.

> But be doers of the word, and not merely hearers who deceive themselves. For if any are hearers of the word and not doers, they are like those who look at themselves in a mirror; for they look at themselves and, on going away, immediately forget what they were like. But those who look into the perfect law, the law of liberty, and persevere, being not hearers who forget but doers who act—they will be blessed in their doing.

Spirit Booster: Reaching In
Take a good look at yourself in a mirror. What do you see? You see a person who is a child of God. Remember that when you look at yourself—even in the morning when your hair is a mess and your eyes are bleary!

Spirit Booster: Reaching Out
Purchase a small, inexpensive pocket mirror. Give it to someone with a note that claims, "When I see you I think about Christ's love."

DAY 2
The Coat

I grew up in southern California, where heavy winter coats were about as necessary as a sandbox in the desert. Not until I moved east to go to seminary did I find myself in need of outerwear a little more substantial than a windbreaker or lightweight sweater.

Shortly after my arrival in Princeton, I took the train to Washington, D.C., to visit my aunt Arlene. Our first order of business: to purchase a coat that would see me through the New Jersey winters. I tried on dozens of coats until I finally found the perfect style, size, and price. Bring on the winter snows!

Through the years, I wore that coat a lot. I also visited my aunt as often as possible. Arlene was the family member I connected with. We looked alike. We had similar interests. She was the first of my relatives to meet my future husband.

After graduating from seminary, Greg and I moved to Pennsylvania. As our children began to arrive, I replaced my first winter coat with others that could accommodate my changing figure and survive the inevitable drool that found its way onto every article of my clothing.

Though distance made my visits with Arlene less frequent, we kept in touch. She stopped to see us one Christmas on her way home to Ohio. A few months later, she arrived within days after the birth of our oldest son.

The following December, Arlene became ill with cancer. She fought a brave fight, but the cancer's ammunition proved greater than what the doctors could offer. Two months before the birth of our daughter, Arlene died at the age of forty-seven.

The coat continued to hang in my closet, unused. After

Arlene's death, I couldn't bear to throw it away. It reminded me of those happy days when the future stretched before us full of hope and promise, and cancer was not in the picture.

I cleaned out my closet on a bitter winter day and came across the coat. Images of Arlene flooded my mind. Sixteen years had passed since I first tried on that coat. For too many of those years, the coat's purpose had not been fulfilled.

I held the coat and thought about all the homeless people who even at that moment shivered in the cold, while my coat hung there, gathering dust.

I took the coat that very day and gave it to a place that distributed clothing to the homeless. I knew that that's what Christ wanted me to do. It seemed a more fitting tribute to Arlene to give the coat away so that someone else could stay warm. Sometimes, living our faith means giving so that another person can receive.

I have a few other keepsakes from Arlene. Mostly, I have the wonderful memories of an aunt I deeply loved, and the knowledge that somebody else has benefitted from that love.

That's enough to keep me warm on a cold winter day.

DAY 3

When someone steals a
   man's clothes
      we call him a thief.
Should we not give the
same name
      to one who could
      clothe the naked
      and does not?

The bread in your
cupboard
    belongs to the hungry man;
the coat hanging unused
in your closet
    belongs to the man
    who has no shoes;
the money which you
hoard up
    belongs to the poor.
        —St. Basil the Great,
        Living More with Less, 13

DAY 4

God, lover of us all,
most holy one,
help us to respond to you,
to create what you want for us here on earth.
Give us today enough for our needs;
forgive our weak and deliberate offences,
just as we must forgive others
when they hurt us.
Help us to resist evil
and to do what is good;
for we are yours,
endowed with your power
to make our world whole.
        —Lala Winkley, *The Complete Book of*
        Christian Prayer, 305

DAY 5
The Clean-Up Club

Week after week, it was the same. Scraps of paper littering the floor. Hymn books scattered along pews. Pencil stubs strewn about like fallen timber. Finally, she'd had enough.

Indignant with the way the church looked after worship every week, this "she" decided to take matters into her own hands. It made no difference that "she" was only seven years old. Once my daughter makes up her mind, there's no changing it.

Amy discussed the matter with her good friend, Elaine. Together, the two of them planned a course of action.

They made a sign-up sheet for volunteers. They set up a table in the church lobby. They came to Greg and me and asked if we, the pastors of the church, would announce in worship that a new "Clean-Up Club" was in the works.

What's a pastor to do? I didn't want Amy to be disappointed when nobody rushed to volunteer for her new club. "Let me think about this," I said, hoping that if I delayed for a few weeks, the idea would pass and she would forget about it. I should have known better.

After three weeks of living with my wishy-washy ways, Amy could wait no longer. The church's disarray wasn't getting any better. Amy might not mind if her room at home resembled the rubble left by a passing hurricane. "Her church" was another matter altogether.

The time came one Sunday morning for the weekly announcements. There, in the front row of the sanctuary, my daughter raised her slender hand. I had no choice but to call on her.

Amy's large, blue eyes shone with sincerity and excitement. "I'd like to invite everybody to join our Clean-Up Club," she piped up, Elaine by her side. "Anyone who wants to help keep the church clean can join. There's a sign-up table by the front door." I watched the faces of the people in the congregation light up like Christmas Eve candles. Amy sat down, unaware of the sea of smiling faces welling up behind her.

When worship ended, I got caught up in the usual frenzy of greeting people, gathering my sermon notes, turning out the lights, and looking for my children. As I came around the corner to my office, there sat Amy and Elaine at their table, big grins on their faces. Ten people of all ages signed up for the Clean-Up Club on the first day of registration.

We all learned a lesson that day about the stewardship of our church property and how it's up to everyone to take care of the gift that our church truly is. Why just talk when you can actually do something?

Once Amy and Elaine got the Clean-Up Club off the ground, they came to me and asked about starting a "Lost and Found."

This time, I listened.

DAY 6

"Half the world is starving; the other half is on a diet. We are not privileged because we deserve to be. Privilege accepted should mean responsibility accepted."
—Madeleine L'Engle, *The Westminster Collection of Christian Quotations*, 318

DAY 7

Breath Prayer: Close your eyes; take several slow, deep breaths; then silently pray this breath prayer in rhythm with your breathing. Repeat several times.

*Let me always be
a doer of your word.*

— Light your Sabbath Celebration candle. Sit quietly for five minutes.
— Read the Bible passage for this week: James 1:22–25.
— Quietly reflect on the joy that comes when you hear God's word, and try to live that word in your daily life.
— How have you been a "doer" of God's word?
— In your journal, write down the ways in which you intend to be a doer of the word, to live out your faith. Make a note on your calendar for November to look back at this list and see if you have been able to carry through.
— Pray for God to challenge you to not only hear God's word but to act on it.

It is the Sabbath that inspires all the creatures to sing praise to the Lord. (Abraham Joshua Heschel, 24)

SEPTEMBER
INTEGRITY

WEEK 1

DAY 1

Read the following Bible passage each day this week: Joshua 24:14–15.

> "Now therefore revere the LORD, and serve him in sincerity and in faithfulness. . . . Now if you are unwilling to serve the LORD, choose this day whom you will serve, . . . but as for me and my household, we will serve the LORD."

Spirit Booster: Reaching In
Substitute time you would normally spend watching a television show and use that time for silence and meditation.

Spirit Booster: Reaching Out
Substitute time you would normally spend watching a television show and spend it with a loved one or family member.

DAY 2
More Than a Nice Thought

We have a plaque hanging near the front door of our home with an excerpt from Joshua 24: "As for me and my house, we will serve the LORD."

The plaque was a Christmas gift several years ago, given to us by a family in the church, who felt like that Scripture passage made a good motto for two pastors and their three kids. I agree, although it's a good motto for any family to live by.

It's certainly a nice thought. But the more I think about it, the more I realize that it is far more than a nice thought. It's kind of frightening, really. How does one go about ensuring that one's family, one's household, will serve the Lord? If we post that claim for the world to see, we'd better be doing our best to be sure that the words are more than a nice thought.

We attend church, of course. We say grace around the dinner table, on those rare nights when we are fortunate enough to actually gather and sit for a meal rather than grabbing a bagel or a slice of leftover pizza on our way out the door to soccer practice or Youth Fellowship or any assortment of meetings and school-related activities.

We even get a paycheck for much of the service we render unto the Lord. But is that the extent of what it means to serve the Lord?

No.

As a clergy family, we walk a fine line between opening our home to the church community and protecting the privacy of our not-so-private lives. Yet we have always sought to have a home where people of any age are welcome to stop in any time, where the high school youth group can spend the night after a dance and thus be in a safe and secure environment. We host a Christmas open house every year, a tradition begun our first year in Wildwood, when we knew that the people were curious about this new clergy family with three very young children, and when we were striving to overcome the congregation's fear of "intruding" upon our lives. We had such a great time that we decided to have an open house every year, and we've done that, except for the time when I ended up in the hospital with emergency surgery four days before the date.

Along the way, our congregation has discovered that we are just the same as everybody else. We get sick, have bad days, grieve, laugh, attend our kids' sports and school events, worry about money. There is dust on our shelves and dog hair on the couch, and our kids go through the same problems as everyone else's. We really aren't much different from the families that make up the bulk of our congregation, and we don't try to pretend otherwise. I think that maybe this, more than anything else, makes it possible for us to say that "as for the Bostroms, we will serve the Lord," just like the rest of you, and hand in hand with you every step of the way.

DAY 3
The Faithful

Up and up the stairs of time
the pilgrims climb . . .
no matter what
one more time
always one more time.
— Ann Weems, *Searching
for Shalom*, 57

DAY 4
Yes

You are the God who is simple, direct, clear with us and
    for us.
You have committed yourself to us.
You have said *yes* to us in creation,
    yes to us in our birth,
    yes to us in our baptism,
    yes to us in our awakening this day.

But we are aware of another kind,
    more accustomed to "perhaps, maybe, we'll see,"
    left in wonderment and ambiguity.

We live our lives not back to your *yes*,
    but out of our endless "perhaps."

So we pray for your mercy this day that we may live *yes*
    back to you,
    yes with our time,
    yes with our money,
    yes with our sexuality,
    yes with our strength and with our weakness,
    yes to our neighbor,
    yes and no longer "perhaps."

In the name of your enfleshed *yes* to us,
    even Jesus who is our *yes* into your future. Amen.
                —Walter Brueggemann, *Awed to Heaven,*
                        Rooted in Earth, 91

DAY 5
Being Intentional

Whenever God is involved, there is a choice to be made.

This truth strikes some as a paradox, at least those whose theological views include God as some giant Gepetto in the sky, controlling the marionette strings that keep us hopping about like that cute little wooden boy, Pinocchio.

God cut those strings when "free will" came into being, which, from all appearances, seems to be right at the very beginning of time.

And although scientists are now studying what could possibly be a "God gene," giving some people a greater tendency towards faith than others, the bottom line still seems to be that, when it comes to faith in God, we have to decide whether to believe or not.

Joshua is the Old Testament fellow who led the Israelites into their new lives as settlers rather than sojourners, after Moses kicked the bucket just this side of the Promised Land. Joshua gave his golden years to being a fair and faithful ruler of the people. Now, Joshua knew his time was about up, and he wanted to be sure that the people didn't turn their backs on God as soon as he left to join Moses in the everlasting Promised Land.

"Choose this day whom you will serve," he tells them. Choose, and then be true to that choice, because it isn't going to be easy. Make your own choice, because unless your choice comes from the heart, what you promise is going to be nothing but a bunch of empty words.

I like the way the Presbyterian church works. We baptize infants and ask parents and guardians and the whole church to love, encourage, and support these little ones. However, at some point in their lives, when they are confirmed, they have to stand up in front of the congregation and make the choice to be part of the church, part of the faith. If they choose not to do so, well, that's their choice. We still love, encourage, and support them. But they have to choose to make their faith their own, and that makes it all the more precious—and real—as the years go by.

"Choose this day whom you will serve." It's a choice you may have to make every day for the rest of your lives. Being intentional about faith keeps it from ever becoming obsolete.

DAY 6

"Compassion and justice are companions, not choices."
—William Sloane Coffin, *Credo*, 51

DAY 7

Breath Prayer: Close your eyes; take several slow, deep breaths; then silently pray this breath prayer in rhythm with your breathing. Repeat several times.

*I choose today
to serve only you.*

— Light your Sabbath Celebration candle. Sit quietly for five minutes.
— Read the Bible passage for this week: Joshua 24:14–15.
— Quietly reflect on the choice you have been given to serve God, and what a wonderful opportunity that is.
— What are the obstacles that keep you from serving God? Time constraints? Too many other activities? A

lack of desire to do so? What do you need to change in your life in order to serve God more faithfully?

— In your journal, write about the conscious choices you have made in your life to serve God, even when it may not have been easy to do so.

— Thank God for the gift of choice, and pray for wisdom to make the right choices.

One must abstain from toil and strain on the seventh day, even from strain in the service of God. (Abraham Joshua Heschel, 30)

WEEK 2

DAY 1

Read the following Bible passage each day this week: Matthew 5:43–47.

> "You have heard that it was said, 'You shall love your neighbor and hate your enemy.' But I say to you, Love your enemies and pray for those who persecute you, so that you may be children of your Father in heaven; for he makes his sun rise on the evil and on the good, and sends rain on the righteous and on the unrighteous. For if you love those who love you, what reward do you have? Do not even the tax collectors do the same? And if you greet only your brothers and sisters, what more are you doing than others? Do not even the Gentiles do the same?"

Spirit Booster: Reaching In
Do you wake up early enough to see the sun rise? Try and do that at least once this week, giving thanks for the beauty of the dawning of a new day.

Spirit Booster: Reaching Out
Invite someone to watch the sunset with you—even if that person is in another state (you can both agree to watch the sun set on the same day!).

DAY 2
Baby Steps

It's bad enough that Jesus talks about "loving your neighbor as yourself." That's a tough order when so many of us don't know our neighbors, and aren't all that pleased with who we are. But loving my neighbor—that's something I can fudge with a bit, especially if I ask the question that the lawyer asks Jesus: "Who is my neighbor?" (Luke 10:29). That always buys a bit of time.

Now, Jesus has to get even more specific.

Love my enemies? Pray for those who persecute me? Are you kidding? Can't I just avoid them altogether?

"Enemies" and "those who persecute you" aren't fully anonymous people. They're the ones who have intentionally done something to cause you pain and distress. Am I really supposed to love the person I thought was a friend but who told my deepest secrets to someone I hardly even know? How am I supposed to pray for my boss who criticizes every single thing I do and makes my life miserable for no good reason at all?

When our "enemies" and "persecutors" have faces and names, loving them and praying for them takes on an utterly agonizing dimension. Didn't Jesus realize this? Did he think it was a simple thing to ask of his followers?

Of course not. Jesus had plenty of enemies and plenty of persecutors. If anyone knew this was a tough assignment, it was Jesus.

Without Jesus, we can't love and pray for those most unlovable and seemingly beyond redemption. Even with Jesus, it's going to be a struggle. Being able to love our enemies and pray for our persecutors doesn't happen overnight. We can start heading in that direction, however, by taking baby steps. You don't have to fully and completely reconcile with your enemies and make them your best buddies. Loving the one who betrayed you may begin with this acknowledgment: "Jesus, I need your help now more than ever." Praying that your own heart has more room in it for love than for hate may be a baby step toward letting go of the bitterness you feel towards your boss.

Think of the process as akin to snow thawing after a long winter. We can't actually see the ice start to melt, the water sinking into the earth or evaporating drop by drop into the air. One day, however, we step outside and there where the snow has almost (but not quite) disappeared a tiny crocus lifts its purple petals to the sun.

And all this time it seemed like nothing was happening. Guess again.

DAY 3

Do not retreat into your private world,
That place of safety, sheltered from the storm,
Where you may tend your garden, seek your soul,
And rest with loved ones where the fire burns warm.

To tend a garden is a precious thing,
But dearer still the one where all may roam,
The weeds of poison, poverty, and war,
Demand your care, who call the earth your home.

To seek your world it is a precious thing,
But you will never find it on your own,
Only among the clamor, threat, and pain
Of other people's need will love be known.

To rest with loved ones is a precious thing,
But peace of mind exacts a higher cost,
Your children will not rest and play in quiet,
While they still hear the crying of the lost.

Do not retreat into your private world,
There are more ways than firesides to keep warm.
There is no shelter from the rage of life,
So meet its eye, and dance within the storm.
—Kathy Galloway, *Bread of Tomorrow*, 66

DAY 4

O God, our Father, you have told us that we must not judge others, if we ourselves do not want to be judged. Help us never to be too critical of each other.

Keep us from harshly criticizing the work of others, and help us to remember that we have no right to criticize anyone's work, unless we are prepared to do the job better, or at least give a hand with it.

Keep us from unsympathetically criticizing the pleasures of others. Help us to remember that different people have different ways of enjoying themselves, that different people like different kinds of music and games and books, and different ways of spending their leisure. Help us not to despise everything which we don't like.

Keep us from contemptuously or arrogantly criticizing the beliefs of others. Help us to remember that there are as many ways to the stars as there are those to climb them; and help us never to laugh at anyone's belief, if that is the way he or she gets to God.

Help us always,
   To praise rather than to criticize;
   To sympathize rather than to condemn;

To encourage rather than to discourage;
To build up rather than to destroy;
To think of people at their best rather than at their
worst.

Amen.

—William Barclay, *A Barclay Prayer Book*, 188–89

DAY 5
For Your Own Good

If there's one thing most people can't stand, it's being told
they have to do something they don't like because it's for
their own good.

"Eat those peas. It's for your own good."

"Take your medicine. It's for your own good."

"Get out and exercise. It's for your own good."

Who needs it?

Usually the thing we're being told to do is utterly dis-
tasteful, else nobody would have to tell us to do it, and
nobody would have to try and justify the telling by saying,
"It's for your own good."

I wonder if Jesus knew this human tendency to balk at
being told what to do because it is good for us.

For instance, when he tells the crowds to love their
neighbors and to pray for those who persecute them, he is
careful not to say, "It's for your own good." Deep down,
however, that's the truth of it.

Holding a grudge, picking at an old wound, harboring
a festering dislike for somebody—even when they deserve
to be felt that way about—hurts the person who has
already been injured, sometimes more than the one who
did the hurting.

Learning to let go doesn't mean that what someone did

to you is "okay." Learning to let go doesn't mean you won't get hurt again. But learning to let go can free you to move beyond the pain in a way that isn't possible as long as your spirit is still bleeding fresh blood.

Learn to let go, as best as you can. It isn't just for the sake of someone else. It's for your own good. And Jesus knew that, I am sure.

DAY 6

"We all belong one to another. That's the way God made us. Christ died to keep us that way. Our sin is only and always that we put asunder what God has joined together."

—William Sloane Coffin, *Credo*, 33

DAY 7

Breath Prayer: Close your eyes; take several slow, deep breaths; then silently pray this breath prayer in rhythm with your breathing. Repeat several times.

*Lord, let me be
your child today.*

— Light your Sabbath Celebration candle. Sit quietly for five minutes.
— Read the Bible passage for this week: Matthew 5:43–47.
— Quietly reflect on the ways that the media reinforces the concept of hating those whom you consider to be your opponents or enemies. What would be different in

the world if everyone lived by Jesus' commandment to love your enemies and to pray for those who persecute you?

— Often it seems unfair when bad things happen to good people. What does this Bible passage say about the fairness of God? Do you agree with the way things are?

— In your journal, write down your thoughts about this Bible passage. Would you change the way the world works if you could, so that bad things only happened to "bad" people? What does this passage tell you about how you are to respond to people who hurt you?

— Pray, as Jesus said, for those who persecute you, and for help in responding to those whom you consider your "enemies."

The Sabbath is a day of harmony and peace, peace between [people], peace within [people], and peace with all things. (Abraham Joshua Heschel, 31)

WEEK 3

DAY 1

Read the following Bible passage each day this week: Psalm 26:11–12.

> But as for me, I walk in my integrity;
>   redeem me, and be gracious to me.
> My foot stands on level ground;
>   in the great congregation I will bless the LORD.

Spirit Booster: Reaching In
Take a walk if you can—and not for exercise, but to enjoy the beauty of God's world.

Spirit Booster: Reaching Out
Tell someone about what you appreciated when you took a walk and took the time to appreciate the beauty around you.

DAY 2
The Star of the Game

Not long ago, my friend Adam played in a basketball game. He played in a Special Olympics tournament with other young men, all of whom were "special needs children." Some of the kids have physical disabilities. Others have mental or social difficulties. Adam has Down's Syndrome, as do others on the team.

Now, Adam is shy and not very aggressive, so when he gets a chance to shoot the ball at the basket, it's a big moment for him. In that particular game, Adam didn't have many opportunities to take a shot. In the final minutes of the game, Adam finally got the ball, but in the course of the play, a boy from the other team was accidentally knocked to the floor. The crowd shouted, "Shoot the ball, Adam! Shoot the ball!" so excited was everyone for Adam to have this chance to make a basket.

But Adam didn't shoot the ball. He saw the other player on the floor, and he stopped, right there, and held the ball. He refused to move until the other boy got up, and Adam knew that he was going to be okay.

Because he had stopped play, the referee had to take the ball from Adam and give it to the other team. If this had been a basketball game at the United Center, or almost any other stadium anywhere else in the world, the crowd would have booed and Adam would have been the goat. Integrity isn't rewarded in a society more interested in winning and losing than in making sure the guy who gets knocked down is going to be alright.

But in this game, it didn't matter who won or who lost. The kids were just happy to have a chance to play.

Adam didn't get another chance to shoot the ball, to try

for a basket. He didn't mind. As far as everyone there was concerned, Adam was the star of the game.

⌒⌒⌒

DAY 3
By Gracious Powers

By gracious powers so wonderfully sheltered,
and confidently waiting come what may,
we know that God is with us night and morning,
and never fails to greet us each new day.

Yet is this heart by its old foe tormented,
still evil days bring burdens hard to bear;
O give our frightened souls the sure salvation,
for which, O Lord, you taught us to prepare.

And when this cup you give is filled to brimming
with bitter suffering, hard to understand,
we take it thankfully and without trembling,
out of so good and so beloved a hand.

Yet when again in this same world you give us
the joy we had, the brightness of your Sun,
we shall remember all the days we lived through,
and our whole life shall then be yours alone.
—Dietrich Bonhoeffer, written in a concentration
camp shortly before his death.*

*_The Hymnal 1982_, #695. Words: Dietrich Bonhoeffer, trans. by Fred Pratt Green. Trans. © 1974 Hope Publishing Co., Carol Stream, IL 60188. All rights reserved. Used by permission.

DAY 4

Holy and eternal God,
in you we live and move and have our being.
In all our cares and occupations,
guide and govern us by your Spirit,
that we may both remember and reveal your presence;
through our Savior Jesus Christ.
　　　　　　　　　—*A New Zealand Prayer Book*, 81

⚭⚭

DAY 5
Watch Where You're Walking

I took a preaching class a number of years after graduating from seminary, as part of a continuing education seminar. I learned a lot of great tips for writing and preaching sermons, but the best advice the professor gave us was always to look for the part of the Scripture text that catches us a bit off guard and grabs us by surprise. I've tried to do that on a regular basis, and I believe I've come to understand many of the biblical texts in a deeper way.

This is true for this week's Scripture passage, Psalm 26:11–12. The writer of the Psalm pleads to God for mercy and justice, and in an attempt to vindicate himself, states that "I walk in my integrity."

I walk in *my* integrity.

Not God's integrity. "My" integrity.

In verse 3 of the psalm, the writer claims to be walking in faithfulness to God. But prior to that the writer begins with the same line as found in verse 11, only stated in the past tense: "I have walked in my integrity." Again, the word *my*.

There is a sense of personal responsibility implied here. The writer understands that faithfulness to God is a requisite for a good and decent life, and hopes that God will recognize that faithfulness and reward it by plucking the writer out of the pit that swarms with hypocrites and evildoers.

Yet the writer's insistence on prefacing "integrity" with the personal pronoun "my" says to me that the writer is doing his share to live as God requires.

It's that personal responsibility that is so often lacking in life. How much easier it is to blame others for our mistakes, to lay fault at the feet of society's ills, or poor parenting, or an increasing abundance of moral decay.

We are responsible for what we do and say, for how we choose to live. I admire the writer of this psalm for understanding that and for not being afraid to say so.

DAY 6

"True humility doesn't consist of thinking ill of yourself but of not thinking of yourself much differently from the way you'd be apt to think of anybody else."
—Frederick Buechner, *Beyond Words*, 162

DAY 7

Breath Prayer: Close your eyes; take several slow, deep breaths; then silently pray this breath prayer in rhythm with your breathing. Repeat several times.

Redeem me
and be gracious to me.

— Light your Sabbath Celebration candle. Sit quietly for five minutes.
— Read the Bible passage for this week: Psalm 26:11–12.
— Quietly reflect on the need for integrity in your life and in the lives of all people. Is integrity a word you would use to describe the way you live?
— Our daily lives can seem hectic, inside out, and unsteady. The psalmist writes about standing on level ground. Do you feel "grounded" in your faith? Does your faith in Christ give you a sense of security?
— In your journal, write about a person of integrity whom you admire.
— Ask God to keep you steady in your walk of faith, so that you will be a person of integrity.

The Sabbath is meaningful to God, for without it there would be no holiness in our world of time. (Abraham Joshua Heschel, 54)

WEEK 4

DAY 1

Read the following Bible passage each day this week:
Titus 2:7–8.

> Show yourself in all respects a model of good works,
> and in your teaching show integrity, gravity, and
> sound speech that cannot be censured; then any
> opponent will be put to shame, having nothing evil
> to say of us.

Spirit Booster: Reaching In
Try to learn a couple of new words this week, and make
them words with a positive meaning.

Spirit Booster: Reaching Out
Be aware of the words you use and the way you use words
when you speak to others. A kind word in place of a hurt-
ful one can make a big difference!

DAY 2
The Meaning of Integrity

Harper Lee wrote one book in her lifetime: *To Kill a Mockingbird*. I guess if you can write one book that well, there's no need to ever pen another.

To Kill a Mockingbird takes place in Maycomb, Alabama, in the 1930s, a place and time where prejudice against African Americans was still acceptable, at least to some folks. Not to Atticus Finch, the local lawyer, who is called upon to defend a black man, Tom Robinson, accused by a white woman of rape. Tom's case is decided before it ever goes to court: He must be guilty. He's black; she's white. Who are you going to believe? The white woman, of course, even if all the evidence points to the certainty of Tom's innocence.

Atticus willingly defends Tom Robinson, even though it puts his family and his own life at risk. His two young children, Scout and Jem, are ridiculed for what he is doing, and though it breaks Atticus's heart, he knows he has to do what his conscience tells him is right.

One Saturday morning, Scout and her older brother, Jem, are walking into town, when their neighbor, Mrs. Dubose, yells out some cruel and nasty comments about their father, Atticus. Later that day, Jem, in a rage, vandalizes the old woman's flower garden. That evening, Scout climbs into her father's lap, as is her evening ritual, especially when she is in need of a little extra comfort. She questions why she and Jem are supposed to keep their heads held high and ignore the hostility that is continually directed their way. Atticus tucks Scout's head under his chin and rocks her.

"Scout," said Atticus, "when summer comes you'll have to keep your head about far worse things. . . . It's not fair for you and Jem, I know that, but sometimes we have to make the best of things, and the way we conduct ourselves when the chips are down—well, all I can say is, when you and Jem are grown, maybe you'll look back on this with some compassion and some feeling that I didn't let you down. This case, Tom Robinson's case, is something that goes to the essence of a man's conscience—Scout, I couldn't go to church and worship God if I didn't try to help that man. . . ."

"Atticus, you must be wrong. . . ."

"How's that?"

"Well, most folks seem to think they're right and you're wrong. . . ."

"They're certainly entitled to think that, and they're entitled to full respect for their opinions," said Atticus, "but before I can live with other folks I've got to live with myself. The one thing that doesn't abide by majority rule is a person's conscience."

—Lee, 104–105

"Show yourself in all respects a model of good works, and in your teaching show integrity" (Titus 2:7). Imagine if we all took that teaching to heart. Imagine if we all stood up for what was right, not popular. Imagine if we were all willing to put our own life on the line in order to try and save the innocent. Imagine if we all tried to live with the integrity of Jesus.

Imagine what the world would be like. We wouldn't even recognize it.

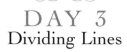

DAY 3
Dividing Lines

How foolish are
the dividing lines

we use to gauge
our rank and worth.

The color of our hair,
when, with time,
it all turns gray.

The shade of our skin
when, like flakes of snow,
no two are the same.

The size of our homes
which should shame us
when there are so many without shelter.

And then there is
the widest dividing line of all: our faith.
"My God is better than your God."

When there is one God,
the God who calls us all children
and in that one word
erases all the lines
we have so carefully drawn.

DAY 4

God of words
God of the Word
Christ who is the Word of words;
Let what I speak
and think
and write,
The words of my mouth

and meditations of my heart,
    be not only acceptable,
        but formed with integrity.
Let the vowels and consonants
        spill forth, unashamed
    that my words may do honor
        to your Word and world.

Amen.

DAY 5
To See, or Not to See

My three children and I looked forward to attending the local children's theater. Every year, our church bought a block of twenty tickets. The parents and children met at a local fast-food restaurant for lunch, then attended the play. That year's show, "The Frog Prince," sounded especially exciting to my amphibian-loving kids.

It's challenging enough to be a "Preacher's Kid," but my three children suffer from a double whammy: my husband and I are both ordained ministers. Most of the time, Chris, Amy, and David benefit from the love and attention of our extended family. But every now and then, the needs of a church member come first.

So when a new member of the church came to me the day of the play and asked if I had any extra tickets, I had to think twice. Should I offer my tickets or tell her, "Sorry, you're too late"?

"Would you mind if we gave our tickets to another family?" I asked my children. "I'll take you to the evening show instead."

"Sure, that's fine," they agreed. "We don't mind. She can have ours."

"Show yourself in all respects a model of good works" (Titus 2:7). My children had done just that. I felt proud of my three kids, so willing to change their plans. The happiness of the mother and her little ones confirmed our decision.

As evening rolled around, so did the thunderclouds. My eagerness to go to the play dwindled with each flash of lightning.

"Let's just stay home tonight," I said. "This storm is going to get nasty."

"You said we could go to the play!" they pleaded. "We really want to go. Please!"

They were right. They'd given up their plans willingly a few hours before. It didn't seem fair they should have to do so again.

We drove to the college and raced to the theater, our umbrella carving a path through the heavy rain. Large signs greeted us: SOLD OUT.

I saw the looks on my children's faces. Had we come this far, only to be turned away? Our jackets soaked and our spirits dampened, I inched my way to the ticket table. "I see the signs," I said. "But is there any chance you have any tickets left at all?"

"How many do you need?" the cashier asked.

"Four," I said.

"Several people had extra tickets and left them here with me," she said, holding up a small stack. Four tickets, exactly.

I got out my wallet. "No charge," she said. "The tickets have already been paid for."

My children and I agreed that it was one of the best plays we'd ever seen. In more ways than one.

DAY 6

"Anger is given to us by God to help us confront true evil. We err when we use it casually, against other people, to gratify our own desires for power or control."
—The monk Evagrius, from Norris, *The Cloister Walk*, 127

DAY 7

Breath Prayer: Close your eyes; take several slow, deep breaths; then silently pray this breath prayer in rhythm with your breathing. Repeat several times.

May I be for you, dear Christ,
a model of good works.

— Light your Sabbath Celebration candle. Sit quietly for five minutes.
— Read the Bible passage for this week: Titus 2:7–8.
— Quietly reflect on how words are used to hurt people. Sometimes, it is the word itself, sometimes the tone of voice used. Even words not spoken can cause pain when one needs to hear a word of kindness or support.
— Do you have a book of poems? How often do you read them? Read some poems that touch your soul. Enjoy the beauty of words, the way they look on a page, the images they draw forth. Treasure the gift of words, as you treasure the gift of the Word, Jesus Christ.
— In your journal, try your hand at writing a poem!
— Pray that you will be a model of good works and a person who uses words to bless.

Creation is the language of God, Time is His song, and things of space the consonants in the song. To sanctify time is to sing the vowels in unison with Him. (Abraham Joshua Heschel, 101)

OCTOBER
TRUST

WEEK 1

DAY 1

Read the following Bible passage each day this week:
Proverbs 3:5–6.

> Trust in the Lord with all your heart,
>   and do not rely on your own insight.
> In all your ways acknowledge him,
>   and he will make straight your paths.

Spirit Booster: Reaching In
Begin and end each day with the words, "I trust in you,
Lord."

Spirit Booster: Reaching Out
Do your best to be a person others can trust (even with
simple things like being on time!).

DAY 2
Anybody Else Up There?

A tourist came to the edge of the Grand Canyon and, leaning over a bit too far, fell over the edge. As he careened

down the face of a cliff, he reached out in desperation and grabbed hold of a scraggly bush with both hands. Frightened out of his wits, he screamed up into the sky, "Is there anyone there?"

A calm voice answered, "Yes, there is."

"Can you help me?" begged the man.

"Probably," the strong voice replied. "What is your problem?"

"I fell over a cliff, and I'm holding on to this bush for dear life, but it's about to give way!" the man cried as the roots of the bush began to pull loose.

The voice above said, "Do you believe?"

"Yes!" the man shouted back.

"Do you have faith?"

"I have very strong faith!" the man called out.

"Then," said the voice, "let go of the bush and everything will be fine."

The man paused, briefly, and then yelled, "Is there anybody else up there?"

It's hard to have faith when the branch is about to break.

Faith is trust—and trust is a concept in which we just don't have much faith.

Every year, good old Charlie Brown trusts that Lucy is going to hold the football in place until he can give it a swift kick in the laces. Every year, Lucy pulls the football away and Charlie Brown ends up flat on his back. Do we admire Charlie Brown for his faith, his trust? No way! He looks like a fool. Why would he trust someone who has never given him a reason to trust? He deserves what he gets! He should know better than to trust Lucy in the first place, let alone after all these years.

If we can't put our faith in someone or something we can actually put our hands on, how can we possibly put our faith and trust in an unseen God?

"Trust in the Lord with all your heart," it is written in the book of Proverbs. But what if God lets us down? What if we trust in God, and our spouse still leaves us? What if we trust in God, and our child still dies? What if we trust in God, and God pulls the football away and we land on our backs, looking like fools?

Faith isn't about having everything turn out the way we ask for it to turn out. Faith is believing—and trusting—that when we fall flat on our backs, or when we're hanging onto a thread, God is going to be the one who reaches out a hand and helps us back to our feet.

How do we know?

God gave us his Word.

DAY 3
I Never Saw a Moor

I never saw a moor,
I never saw the sea;
Yet know I how the heather looks,
And what a wave must be.

I never spoke with God,
Nor visited in Heaven;
Yet certain am I of the spot
As if the chart were given.
—Emily Dickinson, *Eerdman's
Book of Christian Poetry*, 59

DAY 4

Give us courage, O Lord, to stand up and be counted,
to stand up for those who cannot stand up for
    themselves,

to stand up for ourselves when it is needful for us to
   do so.
Let us fear nothing more than we fear you.
Let us love nothing more than we love you,
for thus we shall fear nothing also.
Let us have no other God before you, .
whether nation or party or state or church.
Let us seek no other peace but the peace which is yours,
and make us its instruments,
opening our eyes and our ears and our hearts,
so that we should know always what work of peace we
   may do for you.
                    —Alan Paton, *The One Year Book of Personal Prayer,*
                                              January 11

DAY 5
Finding Our Way

The area where I live is built around several lakes. It's
beautiful, but when it comes to finding your way from one
place to another, it's quite a challenge.

When we first moved to Wildwood, I got lost on a regular basis. If I knew a way to get from Point A to Point B,
I'd take it, never mind that there might be a much shorter
route. I figured it might take me longer, but I'd save time
by not getting lost.

After awhile, I started walking regularly, and that
helped me find my way around. I still got lost, but not as
often.

One day while out walking, a car pulled over and the
driver rolled down her window. She was in tears. "I've
been driving around for an hour, and I can't find my way
out of this place!" she sobbed. Fortunately, I knew my way
around well enough by then to point her in a direction that

would free her from the twisting roads of Wildwood and set her back on a straight and narrow path.

The streets do not run parallel to one another. If you turn right, hoping to find the next street over, good luck. You might end up a few miles in the other direction by the time you realize you're not where you want to be.

The reason the roads are so windy and unpredictable is because of the lakes. Roads and houses are mandated by these beautiful acres of water, which is fine once you've gotten the hang of it. It would be a lot easier to find your way around if the roads were straight and clear.

When I read in Proverbs 3 that if we trust God, God will make straight our paths, I think of that poor woman trying to find her way out of Wildwood. She had no other option right then but to trust me. What a relief it must have been for her to find her way out of the maze and onto a road with clear direction.

What a relief it is to know that, when we are lost in a maze of decisions or of tangled priorities, we can trust God to point us in the right direction.

DAY 6

Trust in the LORD forever,
for in the LORD GOD
you have an everlasting rock.
—Isaiah 26:4

DAY 7

Breath Prayer: Close your eyes; take several slow, deep breaths; then silently pray this breath prayer in rhythm with your breathing. Repeat several times.

I trust in you
with all my heart.

— Light your Sabbath Celebration candle. Sit quietly for
five minutes.
— Read the Bible passage for this week: Proverbs 3:5–6.
— Quietly reflect on the difficulty in trusting others. Is it
any easier to trust in God?
— Have there been times in your life when someone has
broken your trust? Were you ever able to trust that
person again? If so, what made that possible? If not, is
there a way to change that? Does a broken trust with
one person make it harder to trust another?
— In your journal, write down the ways you can be a
trustworthy person. How are these similar to the things
that make it possible for you to trust God?
— Pray that God will help you to be trustworthy and that
you will be willing to put your trust in God.

On the Sabbath we especially care for the seed of eternity
planted in the soul. (Abraham Joshua Heschel, 13)

WEEK 2

DAY 1

Read the following Bible passage each day this week:
Matthew 6:34.

> "So do not worry about tomorrow, for tomorrow
> will bring worries of its own. Today's trouble is
> enough for today."

Spirit Booster: Reaching In
When you begin to feel anxious or worried, take several
deep breaths in and out, until you feel calmed.

Spirit Booster: Reaching Out
Be a calming influence. That may be the best gift a person
can receive when going through an anxious time.

DAY 2
Signs in the Sink

I'd been away at a children's literature conference for two
days. Naturally, before I left, I wore myself out making

sure everything at home was left in near-perfect condition. All the laundry was washed, folded, and put away; the counters were clean and uncluttered; the bills paid; the rug vacuumed; and not a dirty dish in sight. I don't know if I do this so that I can assuage my guilt at leaving my family for short periods of time (I don't think they mind, but I hope they notice!) or if it's because I don't want to come home and have to pick up where I left off, not to mention picking up dirty clothes off the floor.

I attended the conference with a friend of mine whose two children are both away at college. We talked about how quiet her life is now, how orderly her house, how she and her husband actually have time to talk to one another without interruption. These are all well and good, but the deep down truth is that my friend would trade the neatness and quiet for having her kids back at the age where the hustle and bustle of children's activities filled nearly every moment.

When we arrived home, my friend helped me carry my luggage into the house. Nobody was home. My husband and three kids were out and about, as I'd been warned they might be. It felt strange coming into an empty house, save for the dog who wagged his tail with delirious joy at seeing another living being.

For a moment, I bemoaned the fact that nobody was there to greet me. Then I walked into the kitchen. Outrage! Scattered across the counter and piled in the sink were innumerable dirty dishes! How could my husband and kids go out and have fun without first washing the dishes?

My friend heard my shriek of dismay. She gently placed her hand on my arm. "Don't think of them as dirty dishes," she said. "Think of them as signs that there is living going on in this house."

She was right.

Moments later, my family arrived home. We hugged one another, and I caught up on what I'd missed while I was gone. I didn't say a word about the dishes. I left them right where they were.

Funny thing: Later that night, before I went to bed, I made one last pass through the kitchen. There wasn't a dirty dish in sight.

DAY 3
Into the Ordinary

O Amazing God, you come into our ordinary lives
    and set a holy table among us,
filling our plates with the Bread of Life
    and our cups with Salvation.
Send us out, O God,
    with tenderheartedness
to touch an ordinary everyday world
    with the promise of your holiness.
            —Ann Weems, *Searching for Shalom,* 81

DAY 4
Like an endless falling

"Things fall apart,
    the center cannot hold."
We are no strangers to the falling apart;
We perpetrate against the center of our lives,
    and on some days it feels
        like an endless falling,
        like a deep threat,
        like rising water,
        like ruthless wind.
But you . . . you in the midst,

you back in play,
   you rebuking and silencing and ordering,
   you creating restfulness in the very eye of the storm.
You . . . be our center:
   cause us not to lie about the danger,
   cause us not to resist your good order.
Be our God. Be the God you promised,
      and we will be among those surely peaceable in
      your order.
We pray in the name of the one through whom all things
   hold together.
Amen.

—Walter Brueggemann, *Awed to Heaven,*
Rooted in Earth, 26

DAY 5
An Elusive Gift

My life is anything but peaceful: three children and a marriage to nurture, a job whose hours routinely extend beyond their limits, a house to care for, a dog to walk, and an ever-increasing list of publishing deadlines to meet. The days pile upon one another like the mountains of laundry I spend much of my time sorting and stacking and putting away, only to have the next day's load of problems and dirty clothes come roaring down the chute in an attempt to assure that I will never catch up.

When I feel overwhelmed, the best thing I can do for myself (and thus for everyone else who has to live with me) is to head for the sun room. We are blessed to live on a small lake, and we have a small but lovely sun room on the lower level of our home where the lake is visible all seasons of the year.

This portion of the earth, robed in royal blue, shimmers

in the afternoon, stirred by warm fingers of sunlight. I am drawn to the lake, for in its holy presence I find the peace that so eludes me the rest of the day. Perhaps because I grew up near the shores of the Pacific Ocean, my singed soul is quenched by the sight of a large expanse of water.

I think of the words of Francis Thompson: "Know you what it is to be a child? . . . It is to have a spirit yet streaming from the waters of baptism." The waters of baptism, of new life, of new hope, ripple through me as I gaze upon my beloved lake.

The worries of tomorrow vanish along with the concerns of this particular day. Only this moment exists.

In the hours yet to be born, the phone will ring, the e-mail will need to be answered, the bills will clutter my mailbox, and complaints will drift across my desk. The distractions and disturbances of the day will do their best to consume me. But I know that the blue waters of the lake are always there streaming through my soul, creating calm in my chaos, and giving me peace.

DAY 6

"All other days have either disappeared into darkness and oblivion or not yet emerged from it. Today is the only day there is."

—Frederick Buechner, *Beyond Words*, 390

DAY 7

Breath Prayer: Close your eyes; take several slow, deep breaths; then silently pray this breath prayer in rhythm with your breathing. Repeat several times.

*I turn over my worries
and place them in your care.*

— Light your Sabbath Celebration candle. Sit quietly for five minutes.
— Read the Bible passage for this week: Matthew 6:34.
— Quietly reflect on the worries you carry over from day to day. What good can come of worrying? Worry is different from being conscientious. Think about how this is true.
— Read the verses in Matthew preceding this passage: Matthew 6:25–33. Now read them all again, including verse 34.
— In your journal, write down your worries before you go to bed. As you close your journal, offer your worries to God's care.
— In prayer, turn your worries over to God before you sleep.

All week we may ponder and worry whether we are rich or poor, whether we succeed or fail in our occupations, whether we accomplish or fall short of reaching our goals. But who could feel distressed when gazing at spectral glimpses of eternity, except to feel startled at the vanity of being so distressed? (Abraham Joshua Heschel, 30)

WEEK 3

DAY 1

Read the following Bible passage each day this week:
Psalm 56: 2–4.

O Most High, when I am afraid,
    I put my trust in you.
In God, whose word I praise,
    in God I trust; I am not afraid;
    what can flesh do to me?

Spirit Booster: Reaching In
Every day, we carry a reminder of our trust in God. Look at a quarter or another coin, and find the words "In God We Trust." When you need a quick reminder to trust in God, pull out a coin!

Spirit Booster: Reaching Out
Give a coin to a friend and point out that it is a daily reminder in whom we put our trust.

DAY 2
I Put My Trust in You

April 6, 1999.

It is two days after Easter, and I am sitting at O'Hare International Airport, preparing to board an airplane that will take me from Chicago to Los Angeles, and then on to Las Vegas, where my parents live. My mother is having surgery to see if the shadow in her lungs is lung cancer. I am frightened beyond words.

> *When I am afraid,*
> *I put my trust in you.*
> *In God, whose word I praise,*
> *in God I trust.*

I jog down to an airport coffee shop to get a cup of tea. I stand in line, dig the coins out of my purse, then look up at the cashier. His name tag says, "Jesus." I grew up in a community that was heavily Hispanic, so I know it is pronounced "Hey-Zoos." But I like the thought that I am buying a cup of tea from someone named Jesus. It seems like something Jesus would do, serve a cup of hot tea to a woman on her way to spend time with her ailing mother, who has for so many years greeted her with a welcome cup of tea.

I am comforted by this cashier and his name tag. I leave a nice tip in the cup on the counter. You just never know.

> *When I am afraid,*
> *I put my trust in you.*
> *In God, whose word I praise,*
> *in God I trust.*

Soon, I am on the plane heading west. I think about how life is like a trip to the airport—a journey from one destination to another. We think we are in control, but we are not. First class passengers and those in coach, flight attendants, pilots—we are all at the mercy of nuts and bolts and wind chill factors. We may know where it is we want to go, but there is no guarantee that we will get there, at least not without a few scratches, bruises, broken bones, and broken hearts along the way.

When I am afraid,
I put my trust in you.
In God, whose word I praise,
in God I trust.

Life is a journey from one destination to another. At one end there is life, with people we love so much our hearts break with grief at the thought of leaving them behind. On the other end, just past death, there is another life, and people we love so much that our hearts break with joy at seeing them again. And there are the loving arms of God, enfolding us as my parents will soon welcome me, full of love and joy at being reunited.

In God, whose word I praise,
in God I trust; I am not afraid; what can flesh do to me?

I think of Jesus, the cashier at the coffee shop. I think of Jesus, the Savior of the world.

I put my trust in you, O God. I am afraid of what the doctors will find hidden deep within my mother's lungs. I cannot change that. But I can put my trust in you, O God.

Help me not to be afraid.

DAY 3
Recollection

I have a hunch that much of faith
is formed in looking backward,
taking stock, reflecting on what has been, and what
might have been.
Most of the time, you see,
we're far too close to things
to view them properly.
The hassle hustle of the everyday
can blind us to what's really going on,
obscure for us the chasms and the pinnacles
that mark the landscape of our living.
It's only when, and if, we take the time
to glance across the shoulder and reflect,
to pause and ponder where we are
and how we got here, that we can trace
the constant presence of a mystery
that blesses as it wounds,
that turns us inside out and upside down,
that leads us, by a path we did not choose,
toward a hope we hardly knew we had,
a trust that yet endures, despite so much,
a strange familiar grace that touches
everything we touch with promise.
I'll even bet old stammering Moses,
leading his motley crew across that gap
between the waves, had no time to inquire about
who put it there. He just saw a chance
and grabbed it with both hands. Then later,
on the other bank, or deep in the wilderness,
he realized, "So that's what God
was up to all the time!"
　　—J. Barrie Shepherd, *Theology Today* 61 (2004): 360

DAY 4

"God of life, there are days when the burdens we carry chafe our shoulders and wear us down; when the road seems dreary and endless, the skies gray and threatening; when our lives have no music in them and our hearts are lonely, and our souls have lost their courage. Flood the path with light, we beseech you; turn our eyes to where the skies are full of promise."
> —St. Augustine of Hippo, *Prayers for Healing,* 118

DAY 5
An Antidote to Fear

I must have been only five or six years old at the time, but I remember it as clearly as yesterday.

We lived in San Pedro, California, south of Los Angeles. My dad's sister, Christine, was flying in from Ohio to stay with us for awhile. Excited, we all went to the airport to pick her up.

I trailed along next to my mother and father, chattering, my head bobbing from one side to the other as I drank in the hoards of people bustling about, the message boards flashing the times for arrivals and departures of planes, the zippy little carts hurtling down the aisles loaded with luggage and passengers.

Captivated by the noise and bustle, I didn't realize that the man and woman just in front of me weren't my parents, but a couple of strangers I'd never seen before in my life. I had become separated from my family. I panicked.

The fear swept over me like an ocean wave and nearly

knocked me flat. My heart pounding, my body shaking, I turned in circles, desperate to spot a familiar face. No luck. I knew I would never see my family again, that I was doomed to wander the airport for eternity.

Somehow, in the back of my terrified little mind, I remembered seeing a large radar posted on top of a building near where my father had parked the car. I made my way through the crowds like a trout swimming upstream, found my way outside, and looked up in the sky until I spotted the radar, half a mile at least from where I stood.

With the radar in sight, I traversed the acres of cars until I found the one that I knew. The door had been inadvertently left unlocked, and I crawled into the back seat, sobbing.

Now that I am a parent and have "lost" my kids in Wal-Mart, despite being as careful as any parent can be, I have an inkling as to what my parents must have gone through when they realized I was missing. But back then, I only felt the terror of being a little child lost to my world. I haven't forgotten how that felt.

Eventually, I heard someone open the trunk of the car and dared to peek up over the back of the seat to see the most wonderful sight in the world: my father. Later, my mother told me that when my face popped up in the back seat and my dad saw me, he had to hold back the tears.

When we are overcome with fear, trust is not easily obtained, for fear overcomes nearly every rational thought. Psalm 56 reminds us to put our trust in God when we are afraid. It might be worth memorizing these few lines (verses 2–4) for those times when fear grips us by the throat and renders us nearly immobile. God is someone we can rely on always, even when there isn't a radar in sight.

DAY 6

"[T]here is much that we cannot understand, but our lack of comprehension neither negates nor eliminates it."
—Madeleine L'Engle, *Walking on Water*, 94

DAY 7

Breath Prayer: Close your eyes; take several slow, deep breaths; then silently pray this breath prayer in rhythm with your breathing. Repeat several times.

When I am afraid,
I put my trust in you.

— Light your Sabbath Celebration candle. Sit quietly for five minutes.
— Read the Bible passage for this week: Psalm 56:2–4.
— Quietly reflect on God's protecting you when you are afraid. There is nothing greater than God.
— Memorize these verses from the psalm, so that you carry them in your heart to give you strength and courage in times of trouble.
— In your journal, write down anything that is making you anxious, and entrust these to God's care.
— Pray for release from the fears that bind you.

The seventh day is a palace in time which we build. It is made of soul, of joy and reticence. (Abraham Joshua Heschel, 14–15)

WEEK 4

DAY 1

Read the following Bible passage each day this week: 2 Timothy 1:12.

> But I am not ashamed, for I know the one in whom I have put my trust, and I am sure that he is able to guard until that day what I have entrusted to him.

Spirit Booster: Reaching In
Hold out your palms, place in them your trust, and hand that trust to God.

Spirit Booster: Reaching Out
By necessity, children must put their trust in others. Often, that trust is abused. Pledge to give time, gifts, or resources to a children's home or children's hospital. If you are not in a position to give, you can always pray.

DAY 2
Chris's Cross

My eight-year-old son lay motionless upon his bed, his cheeks flushed with a fever that had consumed every bit of his energy. I placed a cool, damp washcloth on his forehead and rubbed my hand softly against his flaming cheek.

I always think the worst when one of my children is sick. Their usual boundless energy is replaced with an almost lifeless quiet. My helplessness as a mother is intensified beyond any level of comfort. I recognize my limitations, my inability to protect the people I hold most dear. I don't like being reminded of my frailties as a parent. I am terrified of losing my children. It happens.

The day crawled past, saturated by the sickness consuming my young son. I could not think clearly, could not keep my mind on anything but the burning body that imprisoned his joyful spirit. I fed him ice chips, read him stories, and watched in silence as he slept. I felt his chest, his tiny heart beating furiously as it battled its invisible assailant. I lowered my ear to his face, straining to hear the sounds of his faint breath. I prayed, "Dear God, please don't let anything happen to Christopher. Please make him well." I prayed for nothing less than my child's health restored.

Late that night, the fever broke. My son's breathing became steady again, and his heart beat at a regular pace. His pillowcase was soaked with sweat. I lifted his head and removed the pillow so that I could replace the wet case with a fresh one. At that point, I saw it.

Tucked under his pillow, Christopher had placed a small, leather cross, the one that he always kept hanging on the post of his bed—to keep him safe, he once told me. Sometime during the day of the endless fever, my little boy found that cross and brought it closer to his ailing body.

I replaced the dry pillow and kissed Chris's cool cheek. Then I tucked the cross back under the pillow, where he could find it in the morning.

DAY 3

I believe in all that has never yet been spoken.
I want to free what waits within me
so that what no one has dared to wish for

may for once spring clear
without my contriving.

If this is arrogant, God, forgive me,
but this is what I need to say.
May what I do flow from me like a river,
no forcing and no holding back,
the way it is with children.

Then in these swelling and ebbing currents,
these deepening tides moving out, returning,
I will sing you as no one ever has,

streaming through widening channels
into the open sea.
—Rainer Maria Rilke, *Rilke's Book of Hours*, 58

DAY 4

By faith I come to you, gracious God,
thanking you for the gift of this day,
and praying for the energy to face the week ahead.

I offer my prayers, spoken and unspoken
trusting that you hear the prayers I keep inside
as well as those I speak aloud.

By faith I trust in you,
even when that trust does not come easily.
Some days I feel stretched to the breaking point
by life's challenges and strains.
Help me turn my burdens over to you
and to others who care about me.
Be it family, friend, or stranger,
there are always those willing to pray for me
if I allow them,
and the Holy Spirit prays
when I cannot find the words.

By faith, O God, I trust
that nothing is impossible with you.
In a world that is torn to pieces day by day
with violence and hatred and greed,
I still pray for peace.
I cannot change the world
but I can change myself,
to be a seeker of peace in my own life
and home and friendships.

By faith I trust
that you will never abandon me
or your world,
In Jesus Christ I see that
neither life nor death will ever separate us
from your love.
In you, O God, I trust;
And in Christ's name I pray.

Amen

DAY 5
Can I Trust You?

There was an article in the newspaper recently about foster children and what happens to them when they turn twenty-one and are no longer supported by the "system."

One young woman, nearing her twenty-first birthday and with a one-year-old child to support, had lived in eighteen foster homes during the course of her life. The article talked about a lot of issues that arise in such difficult situations, and one of those issues is trust.

How do you learn to trust when life teaches you, "Don't get too comfortable here—it won't last"? Trust arises out of stability and repeated, predictable outcomes. A child who continually has to test new waters isn't going to have the word "trust" in her vocabulary, or in her experience.

Placing trust in God is a risk. We are told that God is steadfast, trustworthy, and reliable; but that is not so easy to believe when the world seems out of control—be that the world at large or the narrower realm of one's personal world.

The more times I read the Bible, the more I see that God really is One whom we can trust. Over and over, no matter how many times we mess up, no matter how far we stray, no matter how we test God, God always comes back to us.

Think of the disciple Peter. He is the disciple that seems most likely to follow his impulses. He tries to walk on the water to Jesus but sinks like a rock. He gives the right answer to Jesus' question, "Who do you say that I am?" and then turns around and blows it. He promises never to betray Jesus and within hours is shrugging his shoulders and feigning surprise and claiming, "Jesus? I don't know any Jesus."

But God never gives up on him. After all that, we read in the book of Acts how Peter spread the good news about Jesus when doing so was riskier than ever. He could do that because he had learned to trust God.

Being a trustworthy person—following through with what you say you'll do, being consistent in your responses to others, never giving up hope no matter how bad the world seems—that is something we are called to be as Christians. If we are trustworthy, reliable human beings, then perhaps someone out there—someone like that foster child who is struggling to find her way in an uncertain world—may just learn that "trust" is not yet extinct.

DAY 6

"Trust the past to God's mercy, the present to God's love, and the future to God's providence."
—St. Augustine of Hippo, *The Westminster Collection of Christian Quotations*, 383

DAY 7

Breath Prayer: Close your eyes; take several slow, deep breaths; then silently pray this breath prayer in rhythm with your breathing. Repeat several times.

I know the One
in whom I put my trust.

— Light your Sabbath Celebration candle. Sit quietly for five minutes.
— Read the Bible passage for this week: 2 Timothy 1:12.

— Quietly reflect on entrusting all that you have to God and having God put this in a safe and secure place where nobody can get to it.
— Too often, our lives are bogged down by shame. We learn at an early age to feel ashamed of ourselves. Second Timothy says that if we put our trust in God, we should not be ashamed. Do you carry around the weight of shame? Trust God to release you from shame.
— In your journal, write whatever you want!
— Thank God for taking away all shame and for guarding all that you hold dear.

We must not forget that it is not a thing that lends significance to a moment; it is the moment that lends significance to things. (Abraham Joshua Heschel, 6)

NOVEMBER
GRATITUDE

WEEK 1

DAY 1

Read the following Bible passage each day this week: 2 Samuel 22:47.

> The Lord lives! Blessed be my rock,
>   and exalted be my God, the rock of my salvation.

Spirit Booster: Reaching In
Place a small rock or polished stone in a special Sabbath Box or in a place where you will see it every day, to be a reminder of God, the rock of your salvation. You can even carry the rock in your pocket when you know that you will need an extra dose of strength for the day.

Spirit Booster: Reaching Out
Give a small rock or stone to someone else, and let them know that the rock is a reminder of God, the rock of our salvation.

DAY 2
The Prayer Rock

When my oldest son was around five years old, the craft project for one of his Sunday school lessons was the "prayer rock." The teachers cut circles of fabric and gave one to each child, along with a small, smooth stone and a piece of string. The children tied the stone up in the cloth with the string. Along with the stone was a poem about placing the stone under your pillow, as a reminder each night when you lay your head down to stop for a moment and pray.

The paper with the poem disappeared in shreds through the years, but the prayer rock remains under my son's pillow—even though he is nearly an adult now. Best of all, he still uses it as a reminder at night to stop and pray before going to sleep.

Several years ago, my youngest son gave me a Mother's Day present. This, too, was a rock, although it was the size of my palm and shaped like a heart. He spray-painted the rock with gold paint and wrote a note, "For you, because you have a heart of gold." What mother's heart—whether made of gold or muscle—wouldn't melt at such a sentiment?

I kept the heart of gold on my desk for a few years, then found a good use for it (although using it as a reminder of the love of my child seemed enough). When I hold a Bible study or lead a women's retreat and the time comes for the closing prayer, I always encourage people to pray aloud if they wish, because many have told me they want to learn to be comfortable with spoken prayer. I also try to be sensitive to those who choose to keep their prayers to themselves and lift them silently to God.

Sometimes the closing prayer circle can be awkward.

Did everyone who wanted to pray aloud get a chance to pray? Should I allow more time? What if two people start to pray aloud at the same time? That's not a problem as I see it, but it makes the people offering the prayer stumble just a bit.

I started using the heart-of-gold prayer rock during these closing prayers. We gather in a closed circle, and I begin the time of prayer. Then I pass the rock to the next person. If that person chooses to pray aloud, she does, holding onto the rock, then passes it to the next person when she is through. If she chooses not to pray aloud, she simply passes the rock to the next person.

The passing of the prayer rock works beautifully. The prayer makes a complete circle, and there's something about passing that stone that connects us together in a special way.

One day our morning Bible study met at the home of one of the women, and I forgot to bring my prayer rock. I had brought small, polished stones to give to each of the women as a closing gift, as this was our last Bible study for awhile. When it came time to pray, I picked up one of the little stones and used it for our prayer rock.

The stone felt cool and smooth in my hand. I prayed, then passed it to the woman next to me. It made its way around the circle and back to me. When I took the stone in my hands again, it startled me. The cool stone was warm from the hands and prayers of the many women who had held it during our time of prayer.

I still use the larger heart of gold much of the time, but there is something wonderful about holding a small, smooth stone and feeling it take on warmth as, one by one, the women pray. My own heart is warmed by these prayers. I imagine that God's heart is, too.

DAY 3
I Did Not See Him

I did not see him
    at first
so still and steady,
    sleek and slim,
hiding, watchful, behind
    the reeds.

I did not see him
    until with
long legs lifted,
    he leaned, lilted,
then lurched like lightning,
    his beak a spear.

I saw him then,
    the heron,
great and gray,
    unblinking eye
wings folded in prayer
    crest winking in the breeze.

How many times
    had I missed him,
sliding through
    still waters?
How many times
    had my eyes been open
yet unseeing?

I whispered,
   so as not to startle him:
   "thank you, God,
   thankyouthankyouthankyou."

DAY 4
The Prayer of Hannah

"My heart exults in the LORD;
   my strength is exalted in my God.
My mouth derides my enemies,
   because I rejoice in my victory.

"There is no Holy One like the LORD,
   no one besides you;
   there is no Rock like our God."
                                    —1 Samuel 2:1–2

DAY 5
A Boulder in the Backyard

Not long after I turned five, my parents moved us from a small house in Long Beach, California, to a larger home in San Pedro, about twenty miles north. They bought a house on a corner lot, with a half-acre of land in the back-yard. Because the house was brand new, they had to start from scratch landscaping the huge yard, but they had it planned out in advance: half the yard would be turned into an in-ground swimming pool. The lawn and the surrounding shrubbery would take shape according to the proposed placement of the pool.

When the landscapers came to dig out the dirt to start

on the pool, they discovered an enormous boulder beneath the surface. After much digging and discussion, it became evident that the only way to remove the boulder would be to blow it to smithereens with dynamite. The cost of this quickly turned the pool into one of those dreams that gets put up on the shelf, brought down from time to time to remember and to mourn, then put away again to gather dust. Instead of a beautiful, blue pool, we ended up with a huge expanse of pebbles, prone to share their turf with endless weeds that it became my duty, in part, to try to obliterate.

As a child, I tried to imagine how deep that boulder went. A rock that huge, that heavy, that immovable, right there in our very own backyard, seemed almost mystical to me.

When we want to describe a person who has been a source of strength and stability for us, we often use the phrase "He (or she) has been my rock": strong, constant, immoveable. That's also how King David described the Lord after David had been delivered from the threats of all his enemies: "The LORD is my rock. . . . Blessed be my rock, and exalted be my God, the rock of my salvation" (2 Samuel 22:2, 47).

The landscape of our life is shaped around God as our rock, our source of protection and strength, the One who will not be moved. And it is a great comfort to know that the rock is right there, in our very own backyard.

DAY 6

"True worship from the heart, then, means responding to God's glory and love with our entire being."
—Marjorie Thompson, *Soul Feast,* 55

DAY 7

Breath Prayer: Close your eyes; take several slow, deep breaths; then silently pray this breath prayer in rhythm with your breathing. Repeat several times.

The Lord lives;
Blessed be my rock.

— Light your Sabbath Celebration candle. Sit quietly for five minutes.
— Read the Bible passage for this week: 2 Samuel 22:47.
— Quietly reflect on the many varieties of rocks: smooth, rough, jagged, polished, solid, speckled, striped; rocks in all sorts of colors, shapes, and sizes. How often do you stop and appreciate the beauty of rocks?
— There are a lot of phrases and metaphors using the image of rocks and stones: "solid as a rock," "rock solid," "steady as a rock," "sink like a stone." What characteristics do these display?
— In your journal, write down other images of strength and solidity that could be used to convey the image of God. For instance, "God is a tree with deep roots and uplifting branches."
— Blessed be God, who is steadfast, solid, strong, and unbreakable!

On the Sabbath the spirit stands and pleads: Accept all
excellence from me. . . . (Abraham Joshua Heschel, 18)

WEEK 2

DAY 1

Read the following Bible passage each day this week:
Luke 17:11–19.

> On the way to Jerusalem Jesus was going through
> the region between Samaria and Galilee. As he
> entered a village, ten lepers approached him. Keep-
> ing their distance, they called out, saying, "Jesus,
> Master, have mercy on us!" When he saw them, he
> said to them, "Go and show yourselves to the
> priests." And as they went, they were made clean.
> Then one of them, when he saw that he was healed,
> turned back, praising God with a loud voice. He
> prostrated himself at Jesus' feet and thanked him.
> And he was a Samaritan. Then Jesus asked, "Were
> not ten made clean? But the other nine, where are
> they? Was none of them found to return and give
> praise to God except this foreigner?" Then [Jesus]
> said to him, "Get up and go on your way; your faith
> has made you well."

Spirit Booster: Reaching In
Need a spirit booster? Thank Jesus for one blessing, each
and every day.

Spirit Booster: Reaching Out
Don't take anyone for granted. Say, "Thanks!"

⌒⌒⌒

DAY 2
Thank You Notes

The holidays are coming soon, and I am prepared.

No, there is no artificial Christmas tree waiting to be taken from storage. We don't leave the lights up on our house all year round. Our Christmas cards will most likely go out in January, if we're lucky. But I'm ready for the holidays.

Last year, after the season ended, I stocked up on thank-you cards. Stacks of them. I aim to write thank you's as the Christmas gifts start arriving. That way, by January 1, I'll be ready to start the new year—because, by golly, I can't relax until all those thank-you notes are done.

Of course, this is my dream. I do have the cards, but finished by January 1? Wishful thinking, every year.

In part, it's because I feel as though every card I write has to be personalized, has to address the gift given, has to point out a quality of the giver, has to try to express in just a few words my gratitude for the time and effort put into choosing just the right gift for me or for my family. I'm not bragging. It just seems the least I can do to say thanks.

I have to be careful not to let my thank-you-note writing become a chore, a massive task to crank out just so that I can feel good. A quickly scrawled, obviously obligatory thank you is fairly obvious and diminishes the purpose of a thank you in the first place. Unless a note can convey a heartfelt sense of gratitude, it's almost better not to bother. Almost.

Perhaps that's why the leper who returned to Jesus to say "Thank you" gets a story in the Gospels. It wasn't just a matter of being grateful: surely the other lepers were grateful for being healed, too. But the one leper went out of his way to return to Jesus. He fell down at Jesus' feet and thanked him, his voice trembling with praise. There could be no doubt that the gratitude he felt came bubbling up from the depths of his soul, a soul that had been ignored and hidden beneath layers, not just of sickly skin, but of a lifetime of being treated like dirt.

The other nine lepers got their outer skin healed that day. But the one—he was healed from the inside out.

DAY 3

God speaks to each of us as he makes us,
then walks with us silently out of the night.

These are the words we dimly hear:

You, sent out beyond your recall,
go to the limits of your longing.
Embody me.

Flare up like flame
and make big shadows I can move in.

Let everything happen to you: beauty and terror.
Just keep going. No feeling is final.
Don't let yourself lose me.

Nearby is the country they call life.
You will know it by its seriousness.

Give me your hand.
         —Rainer Maria Rilke, *Rilke's Book of Hours*, 88

DAY 4

"Is not sight a jewel? Is not hearing a treasure? Is not speech a glory? O my Lord, pardon my ingratitude and pity my dullness who am not sensible of these gifts. The freedom of thy bounty hath deceived me. These things were too near to be considered. Thou presented me with thy blessings, and I was not aware. But now I give thanks and adore and praise thee for thy inestimable favours."
— Thomas Traherne, *The Complete Book of Christian Prayer*, 34

DAY 5
Part of a Miracle

Have you ever wished you could have been present at one of Jesus' miracles? Something grand and glorious:

Like the healing of the pack of lepers?
Or seeing Jesus walk across the rollicking waves to a
    boatload of soggy disciples?
Or waving his arms and making that ferocious storm
    settle down quiet as a kitten?

I'd settle for having been at the wedding where Jesus turned water into wine. That could come in handy during the holidays.

How would it have felt to have been among that crowd of over five-thousand people gathered on that sloping hillside as baskets brimming with bread got passed around? Wouldn't it be grand to have been with Jesus that day?

It didn't start out as a day of miracles. Jesus hadn't planned to prepare a feast for a hungry crowd. He wanted to be alone, to grieve the violent and traumatic death of his cousin and friend, John the Baptist.

But solitude was not what Jesus got. Instead, he was given a crowd. A crowd of excited, curious, eager people. Some came to hear him speak, and he spoke just the words they needed to hear. Some who came were sick, and Jesus healed them. Some came simply to be in the presence of this puzzling and amazing man.

At the end of that long, wearisome day, the people were reluctant to leave. Tired and hungry, they stayed. And Jesus didn't have the heart to tell them to go.

It was late at night. Spread across the grass like butter on bread were thousands of eager and hungry people. They'd been that way for hours. There were the sounds of children laughing and crying, bees buzzing, people clearing their throats, stomachs rumbling, perhaps even a few snores. The hot, summer air had been been lifted by a cool, nighttime breeze. Everyone was hungry. But nobody dared to eat.

Some had come in such a hurry that they didn't even think about bringing a brown bag along with them. Some had carefully tucked away a meal in the folds of their cloaks. They were not about to eat, however, because they really only had enough for themselves, and what would they do if someone else asked for a bite? There was not enough to go around. So they all sat there, hungry, hoarding their food if they had it, hoping they could sneak a mouthful when nobody was watching.

The people saw Jesus kibitzing with his disciples. They watched as the disciples shook their heads, then reached into their bags and pulled out a couple of fish and several loaves of bread. Their mouths started to water. Mmmmm. They could taste that bread, that fish. Some patted their pockets, where their own food waited.

Jesus lifted the bread high above his head, so everyone could see it. He offered a short blessing, then broke the bread and gave it to his crew to distribute.

And as the baskets started to make their way through the crowds, a funny thing happened. People reached into their garments and pulled out their own food. They added it to the baskets. They ate. They shared. They passed the food around. They were fed, all those people, all five-thousand plus.

This spur-of-the-moment gathering had turned into the biggest church potluck in the history of the world!

Perhaps the true miracle in this story is that, in the presence of Jesus Christ, in his example of self-sacrifice, in his breaking the bread before them, the people found it in their hearts to stop thinking only about themselves and to feed one another. In the presence of Jesus Christ, a hungry crowd of people who came to see what they could get, ended up giving all they had to give.

We are part of a miracle. We are part of the miracle that in a hungry world, there is plenty of food to share. We are part of the miracles that take place in the most ordinary of acts—like eating, or gathering around a Thanksgiving table with people you love, or hearing beautiful music, or sitting in the pews of a church with other Christians. We can be part of God's miracles, if we allow the presence of Christ to open our hearts.

Have you ever wished you could have been present at one of Jesus' miracles?

You have.

Open your hearts, and you will see.

DAY 6

"If the only prayer you say in your entire life is 'Thank you,' that would suffice."
—Meister Eckhart, in *Looking for God in All the Right Places*, 67

DAY 7

Breath Prayer: Close your eyes; take several slow, deep breaths; then silently pray this breath prayer in rhythm with your breathing. Repeat several times.

Jesus Christ, Son of God,
have mercy on me.

— Light your Sabbath Celebration candle. Sit quietly for five minutes.
— Read the Bible passage for this week: Luke 17:11–19.
— Quietly reflect on the scene in this Bible passage. The lepers see Jesus but keep their distance, because they are "untouchables." They call out for mercy (not for healing!), and Jesus responds. The lepers are healed. One comes back to Jesus, bows down, and thanks him. The other nine do not. Which one of the lepers would you have been? The one who returned? Or one of the nine who did not? Why do you think the one was moved to return and thank Jesus?
— You have much in your life for which to give thanks. Even on the worst of days, there is gratitude to be found and thanks to be given. For what are you most grateful to Jesus?
— In your journal, write a letter of thanks to Christ.
— Offer a prayer of gratitude for the mercy of Christ, who never turns away from human need.

[The Sabbath] is holy not away from us. It is holy unto us. (Abraham Joshua Heschel, 87)

WEEK 3

DAY 1

Read the following Bible passage each day this week: Psalm 118:23–24.

> This is the LORD's doing;
>   it is marvelous in our eyes.
> This is the day that the LORD has made;
>   let us rejoice and be glad in it.

Spirit Booster: Reaching In
Rejoice in the gift of this day.

Spirit Booster: Reaching Out
What can you do to make this a good day for someone? Perhaps rather than "doing" you can focus on "being." Be the kind of person that reflects the joy of Christ.

DAY 2
Special Delivery

When I was a child growing up, life was a lot different from today. I didn't have to walk ten miles to school in a snowstorm, as my parents did—and that's a good thing, since I lived in southern California. I remember a lot of things, but one of my vivid memories is of the different products that were delivered right to our door.

Every couple of days, my mother placed a metal rack of empty, glass milk bottles on the porch, and the Carnation Milk man came and replaced the empty bottles with full ones. It was years before I realized that milk originally came from cows, not from a white paneled truck. The Fuller Brush man brought us our hairbrushes, brooms, and other assorted cleaning and grooming supplies. Even the dry cleaning was picked up and returned directly to our home.

My favorite delivery person was the guy who drove the Helms Bread truck. My brother, sister, and I watched eagerly for the truck to come up our street, a cheerful honk alerting everyone in the neighborhood to the arrival of the bread and pastries that filled the air with that unbeatable smell of fresh baked goods. We figured that truck of bread was a little slice of heaven (okay, pun intended).

Eventually, the glass milk bottles were replaced with cardboard cartons that Mom bought at the store, and the dry cleaning store no longer delivered, and the Fuller Brush man became a thing of the past. When the Helms Bread Company stopped sending trucks of bread into the neighborhoods, we grieved as if we'd lost part of our child-hood—and we had. I'm sad that my own children never got to experience the simple joys that continue to be some of my fondest childhood memories.

We had to trust each week that the milk would be delivered before we needed more, that the clothes would arrive on time, that the brushes and bread would last until the next round of visits. We trusted that each day we would have what we needed, and we did.

In a day and age where we fill our freezers and cup-boards and stock up on king-sized cartons of paper towels, it's easy to forget to give thanks for what we have each day.

Thank you, God, for our daily bread.
Thank you, God, for enough water to drink today's
    portion.
Thank you, God, for the sun rising in the morning and
    setting in the night.
Thank you for this day that you have made.

I still miss the days when milk, brooms, and bread came right to our door. But that shouldn't stop me from being grateful for what each new day brings.

Let us rejoice and be glad for this day that the Lord has made. For each day, as it comes.

DAY 3
New Shoots

Born in the light of the Bright and Morning Star,
    we are new.
Not patched, not mended . . . but new
    like a newborn . . .
    like the morning . . .
The guilt-blotched yesterdays are gone;
    the soul stains are no more!
There is no looking back;
    there are no regrets.
In our newness, we are free.
In the power of God's continuing creation,
    we are:
    new shoots from the root of Jesse,
    new branches from the one true Vine,

new songs breaking through the world's deafness.
This then is a new day.
New shoots, new branches,
 new songs, new day . . .
Bathed in the promise of God's New Creation,
 we begin!
 —Ann Weems, *Searching for Shalom*, 56

DAY 4
This Is the Day

This is the beginning
 of a new day, Lord.
A day unblemished and whole,
 a day full of promises
 and possibilities,
a day untouched by anger,
 sarcasm, or despair.
Give me grace to treasure
 every minute,
to seek you first;
 to reach my hands beyond myself;
to let the warmth of a smile
 crack the ice of isolation;
to be kind to my children
 and the children of my friends,
 and the children of everybody;
to cherish my husband
 and love him anew;
to see the whole day
 through the eyes of my Creator
who also sees this day
 and declares it "very good."

This is the beginning
of a new day, Lord.
I rejoice,
and am glad in it.

DAY 5
Inspiring Eggs

Over the years, eggs have been the source of some of my greatest moments of inspiration.

Remember the TV commercial a few years back, the one comparing drugs to eggs? In it, a pair of hands crack an egg while a somber voice declares, "This is your brain." The camera then focuses on a frying pan: "This is drugs." The hapless yolk and white drop down into the pan, where they begin to sizzle furiously. "And this is your brain on drugs," the same voice continues. End of commercial.

When my eldest son was in kindergarten, he learned about drugs. I'd never even heard of them until I was in high school, but that was a time and place long ago and far away from my own child's introduction to education. He knew only that drugs were something terrible. And he'd seen that egg-drug commercial several times.

One evening, I made pancakes for dinner. Oblivious to any subliminal message I was creating, I cracked a few eggs into a bowl. About that time, my son sauntered into the kitchen. He stopped short, clutching his throat. "Mom!" he shrieked, in a terrified voice, pointing to the eggs. "There's *drugs* in that bowl!" It took me quite a while to calm him down. He refused to eat pancakes for months after that.

Eventually, he got over it, and I was once again making pancakes. I opened the Styrofoam egg carton and reached in to pluck out my victims. I noticed some words written on the inside of the lid. As I banged the first egg against the side of a glass bowl, I scanned the phrase etched across the pale yellow palette. No doubt some plea from the dairy farmers of America about the healthful quality of eggs.

I was unprepared for what I read: "This is the day that the Lord has made; let us rejoice and be glad in it" (Ps. 118:24). I looked again. Did my eyes deceive me?

No. It was indeed the line from the psalm that greeted me. It was a message I needed to hear that day. Maybe one we all need to hear every day. "This is the day that the Lord has made." I had forgotten to rejoice and be glad in it, until I read the familiar words. I finished making the pancakes, but I did so with a deeper sense of awe and gratitude.

Sometimes, when we least expect it, the good news reaches out to us in our most ordinary moments. And in a world where children learn about drugs in kindergarten, we need to hear that good news more than ever.

∽∽ ∽∽

DAY 6

"For joy is to escape from the prison of selfhood and to enter by love into union with the life that dwells and sings within the essence of every other thing and in the core of our own souls. Joy is to feel the doors of the self fly open into a wealth that is endless because none of it is ours and yet it all belongs to us."
—William Sloane Coffin, *Credo*, 123

DAY 7

Breath Prayer: Close your eyes; take several slow, deep breaths; then silently pray this breath prayer in rhythm with your breathing. Repeat several times.

This is the day
the Lord has made.

— Light your Sabbath Celebration candle. Sit quietly for five minutes.
— Read the Bible passage for this week: Psalm 118:23–24.
— Quietly reflect on the psalm's inference that what the Lord does is marvelous and good.
— Try to let go of the concerns of yesterday and the worries of tomorrow, so that you can truly rejoice in *this* day.
— In your journal, write down those worries and concerns and turn them over to God.
— Pray for those who feel no joy today.

The Sabbath is the most precious present [we have]
received from the treasure house of God. (Abraham Joshua
Heschel, 18)

WEEK 4

DAY 1

Read the following Bible passage each day this week: Philippians 4:4–7.

> Rejoice in the Lord always; again I will say, Rejoice. Let your gentleness be known to everyone. The Lord is near. Do not worry about anything, but in everything by prayer and supplication with thanksgiving let your requests be made known to God. And the peace of God, which surpasses all understanding, will guard your hearts and your minds in Christ Jesus.

Spirit Booster: Reaching In
This is the word for the week: ASAP.
    Always Say A Prayer!

Spirit Booster: Reaching Out
Practice gentleness. It is a lost art these days.

DAY 2
In Everything, Give Thanks

Late one August, we received a letter from a friend of ours, Ernie. His eight-month-old granddaughter, Emily, had somehow managed to crawl out of her tightly secured house and to find a way past the protective fence around the family swimming pool. When Emily's mother found her, she was lying at the bottom of the pool, motionless.

Emily was rushed to the hospital. Ernie rushed from his home in Pennsylvania to Arkansas to help watch Emily's two brothers, so the parents could be with their baby daughter as much as possible. He wrote to us about that visit, and in the letter he said,

> I understand how you must feel when you are confronted by grieving people questioning why God permits things like this to happen. People have asked me, "How could such a thing happen to a little baby?" But I have learned much from this situation. I took advantage of an opportunity to sit with my seven- and nine-year-old grandsons, holding hands and talking with God every evening I was with them. We started out each night with, "God, this is the Watson gang again. We want to talk to you about Emily again."
>
> I never prayed with the children before. What a wonderful feeling that prayer time gave me!

And then Ernie added,

> When you get an opportunity in a sermon sometime, maybe you could suggest that people pray in a family environment, not asking for help and guidance,

but just thanking Him for what we have. It would be one of the greatest things that could happen to them. I can attest to that!

After he returned from Arkansas, Ernie learned about two other little girls that fell into swimming pools and survived. One child lives in California; the other, in Florida. Ernie has been trying to find a way to contact these families. "I would like to support those families just as we have been supported within the past three months," he wrote to me. And then he added these words: "Have you noticed every year we have more to give thanks for?"

Every year—even this year, with all that his family has gone through—Ernie gives thanks to God. And he doesn't stop with being grateful for his granddaughter Emily's life. He extends his thankfulness to being able to pray with his little grandsons, and then takes it one step further and seeks to support other families in crisis. The Bible says, "In everything by prayer and supplication with thanksgiving let your requests be made known to God." Sound easy? Anything but. Try praying to God—and just giving thanks—when you are surrounded by the darkness.

> Rejoice in the Lord always; again I will say, Rejoice. Let your gentleness be known to everyone. The Lord is near. Do not worry about anything, but in everything by prayer and supplication with thanksgiving let your requests be made known to God. And the peace of God, which surpasses all understanding, will guard your hearts and your minds in Christ Jesus.
> —Phil. 4:4–7

Hey, Ernie. You're right. It's true. Every day, there is something more for which to give thanks.

DAY 3
Cold Turkey Days

For those who can deny the malls,
and flying footballs on the screen,
there lies, tucked in between the feasting
and those first December days,
a blessed intermission, several hours,
at least, when nothing must be done,
perhaps a little clean-up time,
the daily paper to be read, for once,
from front to back, a walk through woods
or city streets, no matter where,
don't hurry, find a way to see,
a fire to build with branches, log
and flame, then fall asleep beside
a child—yours or your child's child—
to forget time with in play that is
as old as time itself. These,
and a wealth of easy open moments,
wait within the unclaimed hours
of these rarely gifted,
all but holy days.

—J. Barrie Shepherd (unpublished)

DAY 4

God of seed and growth and harvest,
creator of need, creator of satisfaction;
give us, we pray, our daily bread,
sufficient and assured for all.

Give us also, we pray, the bread of life,
and we shall have a care to feed the hungry,
and to seek for peace and justice in the world.
Help us, then, to remember and to know
that you are our life today and every day;
you are the food we need, now and forever.
Amen.

—*A New Zealand Prayer Book*, 125

CO CO

DAY 5
Mope or Cope?

It is the first Sunday of the new year, and I am sitting at home feeling very sad and sorry for myself. I am still on sick leave following the emergency surgery I had in December, and unable yet to attend church.

But what a day to miss! It is the first Sunday of the new year, and I want to be in church to celebrate that. It is Epiphany. We are celebrating communion. And, today is the day we ordain and install new officers in the church — one of my favorite services every year, but especially meaningful this year as my best friend is being ordained and installed as an elder of the church.

And here I sit, in my sweatpants drinking a cup of tea and trying to hold back the tears.

As I sit, I think, "Well, that's one of my options. Sit here and feel sorry for myself." So I do for awhile.

And then I think, "There are other ways of dealing with this."

The best way I can think of to deal with not being present at church this morning is to be present — in spirit, at least. I can take this time to pray, and name each person being ordained and installed in my prayers, and ask God to bless them during this special occasion and during the months and years ahead as they accept God's call to be leaders and servants of the church.

I can give thanks that I am able to pray.

I can give thanks that I am home, in my sweatpants with a cup of tea, and not still in the hospital in those ridiculous gowns and with an IV in my arm.

I can give thanks that even though I cannot be in church today, that does not make me any less a pastor to my people.

It feels a lot better to pray than to sit here and mope.

I guess this applies to any situation, not just this particular Sunday. When we're feeling down, or sad, or sorry for ourselves, or discouraged, or alienated, or lonely, or frustrated—what we need to do is to pray!

We can mope, or we can cope. Or we can go one step further: pray. The Bible does tell us to bring everything to God in prayer. Even a preacher should figure that out.

DAY 6

"Most of all, Sabbath celebration gives us a deep sense of the Joy that is ours because of the resurrection of Christ, and that festival Joy equips us to glorify God in whatever tasks we might undertake in the following six days."
—Marva J. Dawn, *Keeping the Sabbath Wholly*, 200

DAY 7

Breath Prayer: Close your eyes; take several slow, deep breaths; then silently pray this breath prayer in rhythm with your breathing. Repeat several times.

Rejoice in the Lord always,
again I will say, rejoice.

— Light your Sabbath Celebration candle. Sit quietly for five minutes.
— Read the Bible passage for this week: Philippians 4:4–7.
— Quietly reflect on the difference between "joy" and "happiness." Can you have joy even when you are unhappy? Which word best describes the way you view your life?
— The Bible says to "let your requests be made known to God" by "prayer and supplication." Do you feel as though you can tell God anything? Ask for anything? Expect answers to your requests? Does the thought of praying with an attitude of thanksgiving change your response in any way?
— In your journal, ask God whatever you wish, beginning each petition with the words, "With thanksgiving, I ask this prayer. . . ."
— In addition to whatever you pray about, take time not just to ask but to listen to God.

The seventh day is a mine where spirit's precious metal can
be found with which to construct the palace in time, a
dimension in which the human is at home with the divine.
(Abraham Joshua Heschel, 16)

DECEMBER
INCARNATION

WEEK 1

DAY 1

Read the following Bible passage each day this week: Jeremiah 33:14–15.

> The days are surely coming, says the LORD, when I will fulfill the promise I made to the house of Israel and the house of Judah. In those days and at that time I will cause a righteous Branch to spring up for David; and he shall execute justice and righteousness in the land.

Spirit Booster: Reaching In
Add a small branch to your Christmas decorations this year. Place it where you will be reminded of the Bible verses from Jeremiah and the fulfillment of God's promise in Jesus Christ.

Spirit Booster: Reaching Out
Find out when Hanukkah will be celebrated this year. What are the roots of this holiday, and what does it mean to the Jewish people?

DAY 2
The Giving Tree

I'm used to having trees around me: from the enormous banana and eucalyptus trees in the yard of my childhood home in southern California, to the willow bowing its weeping branches into the waters of the lake at the end of our yard here in northern Illinois. When we lived in western Pennsylvania, the trees covered the hillsides like a thick, beautiful carpet—especially evident in the fall when the leaves blazed with brilliant colors. My life has always been filled with trees.

Where would we be without trees?

One of my favorite books is *The Giving Tree*, by Shel Silverstein. It's the story of a tree who would do anything for the little boy who first comes to play in the tree's branches. The tree provides shelter, shade, food, and, eventually, its life, when the boy, now a grown man, chops it down for lumber. Yet, in the end, the tree is still happy, for its stump provides a place for the boy to sit and rest when he becomes a tired and old man.

I don't usually think of a tree as a Christ figure, but in this story a case could certainly be made.

The "righteous branch" that will spring up for David (Jer. 33) is not just a Christ figure; it is Christ, the Messiah that the people await. Even the image of a branch springing up implies that there is still a lengthy time of waiting ahead. Trees don't appear overnight. They take years and years to grow. The first branches of a tree might give a place of rest to a lightweight bird, but they are not prepared for holding up playhouses or climbing children. Fragile branches yet close to the earth may give shade to a caterpillar, but it will be a long time before a weary traveler will find any comfort in its shadows.

But the branch will come forth, and that is good news to a people who have watched the stump to see if there is any life left within it. The branch will come forth, and a tree shall grow, and it will provide shelter for the lonely and food for the hungry and shade for those who are weary and beaten down.

For the tree that grows from the branch that springs forth is no less than the Savior who will do anything—yes, even give his life—for the children of God.

∽∾∽

DAY 3
Unto Us a Son Is Given

Given, not lent,
And not withdrawn—once sent,
This Infant of mankind, this One,
Is still the little welcome Son.

New every year,
New born and newly dear,
He comes with tidings and a song,
The ages long, the ages long;

Even as the cold
Keen winter grows not old,
As childhood is so fresh, foreseen,
And spring in the familiar green.

Sudden as sweet
Come the expected feet.
All joy is young, and new all art,
And he, too, whom we have by heart.
—Alice Meynell, *Eerdmans Book
of Christian Poetry,* 74

DAY 4

Creator God,
We praise you for your love in coming to us,
unworthy though we are.
Give us grace to accept the Christ who comes in your
    name,
and the courage to be Christ for others.

We praise and thank you, Creator God,
for you have not left us alone.
Each year you come to us, Emmanuel,
God with us in a manger.
Each time you come to us
in the broken bread and the cup we share.
In time or out of time you will be revealed
and we shall see you face to face.

Give us courage, God our strength,
to see your Christ in all who suffer,
to be hands to the helpless,
food for the hungry,
and rescue for the oppressed.

Amen.

—A New Zealand Prayer Book, 525–26

DAY 5
Shelf Life

As consumers, we are warned to be cognizant of the shelf life
of perishable products. The shelf life is a safety precaution to

keep us from eating foods that are no longer safe, due to ingredients that only stay fresh for a certain amount of time.

It always feels a bit strange buying food that doesn't have a shelf life listed. Does that mean that the preservatives in those hotdogs are so potent that they will outlive even my great-grandchildren, when I don't yet have any grandchildren? Scary thought (the food, not the grandchildren).

A shelf life is meant for our protection, and for that, I am grateful.

But I'm also glad that there are plenty of life-giving aspects of life that don't have a shelf life.

Imagine if, in our wedding vows, we only had to promise to love the other person for a certain period of time, after which we would be allowed and even encouraged to toss our spouse into the trash. Some folks may treat marriage that way, but it isn't supposed to happen.

Or what if our newborn child came with a shelf life? True, some kids get awfully spoiled, but that doesn't mean they are ever disposable.

Certain virtues are not meant to have limited life spans, either. Truth is one example. A promise is another.

Promises are made to be kept, to last forever. "Forever" means even beyond our own limited life spans. I discovered that after my mother died. Her love for me didn't end when her life did. I still feel her love years later, and I hope that I will for the rest of my life.

When God makes a promise, it's forever. The difficult part is that sometimes we don't see the fulfillment of that promise and assume that it hasn't come true, when in fact it just hasn't been completed. We are still part of the promise, or at least the process of the promise, and that's just as important as the final outcome.

God promised Abraham and Sarah that they would have descendants as plentiful as the stars or the grains of sand. There was no way Abraham and Sarah could live to see that promise fulfilled. They had to believe that the birth of Isaac was enough to show that the promise was in motion. The rest would come long after Abraham and Sarah had turned back into dust.

The prophet Jeremiah promises the people that the Lord will send a Savior, a "righteous Branch" to bring justice and righteousness to the land. The people hold on to that promise, hoping for a better life some day, but they will not be around when it happens. The promise is fulfilled many years down the road when a young girl gives birth to her firstborn son and wraps him in bands of cloth and lays him in a manger.

Even then, the promise has a long way to go. One thing is for certain, however. If God makes a promise, God will keep that promise, however long it takes. Divine love has no shelf life. Maybe that's because a shelf life is reserved for those things that are perishable.

DAY 6

"Why would God—the Holy, Righteous, and Pure—choose to enter the messy circumstances of our perverse and distorted humanity? Evidently the divine eye sees through a different lens than we expect."
—Marjorie Thompson, *Soul Feast,* 124

DAY 7

Breath Prayer: Close your eyes; take several slow, deep breaths; then silently pray this breath prayer in rhythm with your breathing. Repeat several times.

The days have come;
God's promise is fulfilled.

— Light your Sabbath Celebration candle. Sit quietly for five minutes.
— Read the Bible passage for this week: Jeremiah 33:14–15.
— Quietly reflect on Advent as a time of waiting, not only for the Christ to be born but also for that time when Jesus will return in glory.
— Read the first chapter of Matthew, which gives the genealogy of Jesus. What names do you recognize? Think about the many generations of people who waited for Christ to come into the world. Add your name to the genealogy.
— In your journal, write down what you expect from this Advent season. What promises are you hoping to have fulfilled?
— Pray for victims of crime and war, and for justice in the world.

[The Sabbath] is a moment of resurrection of the dormant spirit in our souls. (Abraham Joshua Heschel, 66)

WEEK 2

DAY 1

Read the following Bible passage each day this week: Luke 1:39–45.

> In those days Mary set out and went with haste to a Judean town in the hill country, where she entered the house of Zechariah and greeted Elizabeth. When Elizabeth heard Mary's greeting, the child leaped in her womb. And Elizabeth was filled with the Holy Spirit and exclaimed with a loud cry, "Blessed are you among women and blessed is the fruit of your womb. And why has this happened to me, that the mother of my Lord comes to me? For as soon as I heard the sound of your greeting, the child in my womb leaped for joy. And blessed is she who believed that there would be a fulfillment of what was spoken to her by the Lord."

Spirit Booster: Reaching In
Study some art depicting the visit between Mary and Elizabeth, or the visit by the angel telling Mary that she would give birth to the Son of God.

DAY 2
In Those Days

"In those days Mary set out and went with haste to a Judean town in the hill country where she entered the house of Zechariah and greeted Elizabeth . . ." (Luke 1:39).

In those days.

In what days?

In those days when she knew without a doubt that the words of the angel had come true. She was pregnant. About three months along. Just starting to show.

In those days when Joseph was still trying to sort out what all this meant in his life. When family and friends questioned why he didn't just ditch Mary and find someone else.

In those days when she realized that something miraculous was taking place. Within her life. Within the world.

In those days when it dawned on her that her own plans for the future had been unalterably changed.

In those days, she set out on foot and made the 100-plus-mile journey to her relative Elizabeth's house. Mary had to get out of Nazareth, away from the accusing eyes and tangled-up wedding plans and curious questions. In those days, when she just needed to spend a little time with someone who would not judge, accuse, question, or condemn.

We all have "those days," when life isn't following the course we expected, when our burdens seem to have gained weight overnight, when nothing makes sense anymore, when we long more than anything simply to be welcomed with open and nonjudgmental arms.

I do not know how Mary knew Elizabeth would be just the person she needed. Did she know about Elizabeth's secret pregnancy? Maybe. Maybe not. Somehow, God guided Mary to the home of the one person she most needed to see "in those days."

Is it one of "those days" for you right now? Who is the one person you know you can go to, who will love you no matter what?

And how can you be Elizabeth to a friend or family member who seeks a safe haven in the comfort of your presence?

Being an "Elizabeth" to another person may be the best gift you ever give. It might be the best you ever receive, too.

DAY 3

O dying souls, behold your living spring;
O dazzled eyes, behold your sun of grace;
Dull ears, attend what word this Word doth bring;
Up, heavy hearts, with joy your joy embrace.
From death, from dark, from deafness, from despairs,
This life, this light, this Word, this joy repairs.
—Robert Southwell, *Eerdmans Book
of Christian Poetry*, 19

DAY 4

"Lord Jesus, this Christmas as we sing the familiar carols, hear the familiar readings and ponder on familiar mysteries, give to us the gift of pure worship—that ability which Mary had of attributing to you your true worth, your full value, your inestimable greatness.

Teach us to be reverent; yet teach us how to express the love that burns within our hearts as we think of your goodness to us — that you have come to be our light in darkness, our hope in despair, our strength in weakness, our shelter in the storm — yes, and our eternal Saviour."

— Joyce Huggett, *The Complete Book of Christian Prayer*, 376

DAY 5
Too Close to Call

The Gospels never say a word about Mary's parents. What were they like, I wonder? Did she have brothers or sisters? Was there anyone she felt close enough to talk with when the angel dumped the shocking news on her about her impending motherhood? Did they stand by Mary when the neighbors began whispering behind her back, when the wedding plans were put on hold?

If so, there is nothing in the Gospels to show this. Mary's hasty trip to see Elizabeth makes it sound like she had to get away, far away, to find someone with whom she could speak openly and honestly.

There are times when it is easier to talk with people we don't know than with people we do. Chances are, Mary and Elizabeth hadn't had much — if any — contact during Mary's young life. The distance between them in miles would have been enough to see to that. And they were of completely different generations. Elizabeth was old enough to be Mary's mother, if not her grandmother.

It can be true that the people closest to us have the most difficult time seeing us. Perhaps Mary's mother was more concerned over her daughter's health, or her ruined chances to make a good marriage, than she was over the fact that her daughter's womb housed the Savior of the world. Maybe her sister rubbed her feet when they swelled and her back when it ached, while keeping an eye out for more unannounced angels coming to call. Perhaps Mary's immediate family were too close to see that this young woman—this girl, really—had what it took to be God's chosen one. In their eyes, Mary was a daughter first, a God-bearer second. It doesn't really matter, I suppose, but it is interesting to think about.

The incarnation is a difficult if not impossible concept to grasp. Mary's family may have been the first to wrestle with this theological truth, but they were certainly not the last. The debate has raged ever since: How can Jesus be God and human at the same time?

Advent is a good time to revisit this question. In Advent, we celebrate the coming of Christ as an infant, exemplifying his human side. We also remember that Jesus will come again to the world in splendor and glory, in a way that makes his divinity undeniable. Jesus as human and divine: that's the focus of Advent.

I feel for Mary's parents, and her siblings if she had any. What were those months of preparation like for them?

What is this time of preparation like for you?

DAY 6

"There is nothing so secular that it cannot be sacred, and that is one of the deepest messages of the Incarnation."
—Madeleine L'Engle, *Walking on Water*, 50

DAY 7

Breath Prayer: Close your eyes; take several slow, deep breaths; then silently pray this breath prayer in rhythm with your breathing. Repeat several times.

*Blessed are we
when we believe.*

— Light your Sabbath Celebration candle. Sit quietly for five minutes.
— Read the Bible passage for this week: Luke 1:39–45.
— Quietly reflect on the differences between Mary and Elizabeth (ages, circumstances, responses to the news of impending motherhood). Next, reflect on their similarities. With whom do you most relate: Mary or Elizabeth? Why?
— In your journal, write down the ways in which you feel blessed by God.
— Pray for women who long for children but cannot become pregnant, and for those women who face an unwanted pregnancy.

*One must be overawed by the marvel of time to be ready to perceive the presence of eternity in a single moment.
(Abraham Joshua Heschel, 76)*

WEEK 3

DAY 1

Read the following Bible passage each day this week:
Psalm 98:4–6.

> Make a joyful noise to the LORD, all the earth;
> break forth into joyous song and sing praises.
> Sing praises to the LORD with the lyre,
> with the lyre and the sound of melody.
> With trumpets and the sound of the horn
> make a joyful noise before the King, the LORD.

Spirit Booster: Reaching In
Play some Advent or Christmas music and sing along,
even if you think of your singing as "making a joyful
noise!"

Spirit Booster: Reaching Out
Invite someone over to share a cup of tea and some beautiful music.

DAY 2
A Joyful Noise

When my youngest son was about eight years old, he asked me a lot of questions about heaven. He wanted to know how people kept from getting bored with eternal life that goes "on and on and on." I think he might also have been somewhat concerned about having to spend eternity singing in the heavenly choir. By that age, singing in a choir—something he only did at church—had already lost its appeal, but at least it was only an occasional occurrence, not something he had to do for the rest of his life.

I don't know what angels sound like when they sing. The "angels" that sing at church are two to four years old, and we all think they sound delightful. I don't think that's what Luke had in mind when he wrote about the "multitude of the heavenly host" praising God to the shepherds, but who knows? It must have been a grand and glorious sound that filled the sky that night, at least the sky over the fields dotted with sheep. Funny that the rest of Bethlehem didn't hear the thunderous roar of that heavenly chorus.

I will never be accused of having the voice of an angel when I sing, but I can relate to making a "joyful noise" to the Lord. That's about the nicest thing that can be said for my singing—that it is akin to noise, albeit joyful when I'm singing in church. Psalm 98 reassures me that it's okay not to have a voice like Barbara Streisand. We all have different gifts and are different parts of the body, after all. But if we are going to make noise, let it be joyful noise at that!

Whatever the angels sound like when they sing—whether or not they divide into four-part harmonies or sing a capella—we will probably never know until we need to, and then we won't be able to tell anyone else. I do believe, however, that the sound of singing angels is full of such joy that it will fill eternity and not be at all boring.

<hr>

DAY 3
December Solstice — Dawn

Bracken and grass
all rimed in glacial white
lend almost-neon frosted radiance
to this last dawn before the turning.
Things reverse somehow today.
This wintered world swings back,
without even a momentary lurch,
toward the sun and April.

Following prayers, I gaze once more
beyond the advent candles' glow,
the criss-cross lattice of my study window.
Words from the old Nicene still linger,
. . . I look for the resurrection of the dead . . .
Not much light for looking in, I murmur —
as the first rays brush their glory
to the highest tips of naked branches —
this shortest day will quick be dark again.

Yet brightness hovers out there at the brink
timing its steady, slow returning.
> —J. Barrie Shepherd, *Christian Century*
> (December 27, 2003)

DAY 4

The whole world waits in December darkness
    for a glimpse of the Light of God.
Even those who snarl "Humbug!"
    and chase away the carolers
    have been seen looking toward the skies.
The one who declared he never would forgive
      has forgiven,
    and those who left home
      have returned,
    and even wars are halted,
      if briefly,
    as the whole world looks starward.
In the December darkness
    we peer from our windows
        watching for an angel with rainbow wings
        to announce the Hope of the World.
        —Ann Weems, *Kneeling in Bethlehem,* 15

DAY 5
Lullaby on the Loudspeakers

Advent is a busy time in the life of anyone, let alone a pastor. A hospital was the last place I had planned to be during December, except to visit. But my body decided otherwise. In December of 2001, without any choice in the matter, I lay under the surgeon's knife for the second time that year.

A hospital is not a place to go for quiet and rest. It is anything but a peaceful place. I had a roommate who smoked in the bathroom and turned the lights and TV on in the middle of the night with no regard for my feeble attempts to sleep. Across the hall, an elderly woman with no idea where she was howled with pain and cried for help at least once every three minutes, day and night, day and night, day and night.

Without warning, a "code blue" sent emergency personnel and crash carts racing down the halls. And there was the ever-present beep-beep-beep of IV monitors and heart machines, and the loud conversations of medical personnel and visitors who didn't realize how loudly voices echo off hospital walls and bare floors.

One night as I lay in my hospital bed, hooked up to so many machines I couldn't even move without help and close to tears from the pain and the frustration, I heard a faint sound. Amidst the cries of pain and blaring TVs and beeping monitors, there was another sound so very different from all the others: a soft, sweet song. It was gone as suddenly and as quickly as it had come.

A few hours later, still awake and trying to block out the sounds of the woman wailing across the hall and the loud, angry voice of my roommate, swearing on the telephone, I heard the strange, beautiful sound again. Could it possibly be? No, I must be hearing things.

When the nurse came in to check my vitals, I asked her: Was it the medication I was on, causing me to hear things? Or was there indeed a very different sound breaking through the harshness of that place?

"Oh," she said, as she wrapped the blood-pressure cuff around my bruised arm. "It's a tradition here. Every time a baby is born in the nursery, they play a lullaby on the loudspeakers."

A lullaby on the loudspeakers.

Floating through the harshness of those halls, a lullaby.

And right then, for the first time since I had come through the emergency room of that hospital, I smiled.

I felt hopeful.

I felt peace.

Lullaby on the loudspeakers: a baby is born!

During the remaining time I spent in the hospital, I listened for the sound of that lullaby. Amidst the horrible sounds of pain and misery that surrounded me, I strained to hear the sound of hope, of life, of a new beginning. Lullaby on the loudspeakers. A child is born.

And I thought of another lullaby, which broke into the sounds of the night nearly two-thousand years ago, and in my heart I heard the whisper of angels' wings: "Do not be afraid; for see — I am bringing you good news of great joy for all the people; to you is born this day in the city of David a Savior, who is the Messiah, the Lord" (Luke 2:10–11).

Do not be afraid, for over the sounds of people weeping and IVs beeping and bombs bursting, over the cries of pain and suffering and sorrow, there is a heavenly lullaby: Do not be afraid — I bring you good news, which is for all people.

I wonder sometimes why so few people heard the news of Christ's birth; why only one band of shepherds heard the voice of the angel and the multitude of the heavenly host; why only a few wise men knew to follow the star; why, among the hundreds of people in Bethlehem that night, only a few wondered at what the shepherds told them.

And I think the answer is right there in the words of the Scripture, which tell us that "Mary treasured all these words and pondered them in her heart" (Luke 2:19).

The lullaby of good news that breaks into the world cannot be seen with the eyes or heard with the ears or understood with the mind; it can only be understood when we treasure the words and ponder them in our heart.

The good news can only be understood when we allow it to seep into the broken places where we are most in need of healing. It is not into a world of peace that we need

Christ to be born, but into a world in need of peace. Lullaby on the loudspeakers—unto us is born this day a Savior, who is Christ the Lord. Silent night. Holy night.

It was anything but a silent night, for breaking through the ordinary sounds of life and death there was the rush of wings, the stumbling steps of shepherds, the soft cries of a baby, the sound of God singing to the world a lullaby to announce the birth of his only Son: Good news! Good news. The Savior of the world is born. Emmanuel, God-with-us.

Lullaby on the loudspeakers! Jesus Christ is born!

DAY 6

"If we had a keen vision and feeling of all ordinary human life, it would be like hearing grass grow and the squirrel's heart beat, and we should die of the roar that lies on the other side of silence."
—George Eliot, *Middlemarch*, 177–78

DAY 7

Breath Prayer: Close your eyes; take several slow, deep breaths; then silently pray this breath prayer in rhythm with your breathing. Repeat several times.

Make a joyful noise
all the earth!

— Light your Sabbath Celebration candle. Sit quietly for five minutes.
— Read the Bible passage for this week: Psalm 98:4–6.

— Quietly reflect on the words of the psalm while listening to soft, joyful music.
— What is your favorite Christmas carol? What memories do you have associated with this carol? Why is this one your favorite?
— In your journal, write down the names of people you know who have experienced a difficulty or sorrow this past year. Pray for each of them by name, remembering that the holidays can be particularly painful for many people.
— Thank God for the gift of music, the joy it brings, and the way that music can evoke special memories.

Our world is a world of space moving through time —from the Beginning to the End of Days. (Abraham Joshua Heschel, 97)

WEEK 4

DAY 1

Read the following Bible passage each day this week:
Hebrews 2:17.

> Therefore [Jesus] had to become like his brothers
> and sisters in every respect, so that he might be a
> merciful and faithful high priest in the service of
> God, to make a sacrifice of atonement for the sins of
> the people.

Spirit Booster: Reaching In
Christmas day will soon be here. What gift do you offer
the Christ child this year?

Spirit Booster: Reaching Out
For each new gift you receive, donate a new or gently used
item to a charity. Or offer to wrap gifts for someone who
is sick, or for a family with a new baby, or for an older
adult who could use the help.

DAY 2
Sibling Rivalry

The traditional Christmas card, signed and sealed without much fanfare, seems to be becoming a thing of the past. Nowadays, we receive more Christmas letters than we do cards, taking this time of year to consolidate the year's activities onto one page and sending this synopsis to everyone on our mailing list.

I enjoy receiving the Christmas letters, which update us on the lives of family and friends we wouldn't hear about otherwise. Yet it often seems as though the letters are a litany of accomplishments more than anything else. Yes, these accomplishments are important, but what does this say about what we deem to be important?

What about highlighting the specific personality traits that make our families unique? "Sarah has a kind and gentle spirit, always thinking of others; and Jeremy has such a wonderful sense of humor, he makes us laugh all the time." Including the attributes about our family members we most love and appreciate imbues those qualities with a sense of value and worth. We are who we are not because of what we do, but because of who we are.

When the Scripture speaks of Jesus being "like his brothers and sisters in every way," I start to imagine a lot of sibling rivalry: bickering over who had to take out the trash first, or who got the best grades, or who was the most athletic. Perhaps it would be more appropriate to consider the qualities of character, the conscientiousness and compassion that are human characteristics as well. If Jesus became like his brothers and sisters, this interpretation makes a lot of sense.

We are created in the image of God, but that doesn't mean we have God's nose or bone structure. It means we have the wonderful attributes of God: wisdom, kindness, creativity, reason, and all the other qualities that make us different from the rest of God's creation.

Jesus became like us in every way. That's why we are to try and become like Jesus in every way.

Jesus succeeded in this. We never will. There's only room enough in the world for one Messiah. Fortunately for us, there is room in that Messiah's heart for every single one of us.

DAY 3

Among the oxen (like an ox I'm slow)
I see a glory in the stable grow
Which, with the ox's dullness might at length
    Give me an ox's strength.

Among the asses (stubborn I as they)
I see my Saviour where I looked for hay;
So may my beastlike folly learn at least
    The patience of a beast.

Among the sheep (I like a sheep have strayed)
I watch the manger where my Lord is laid;
Oh that my baa-ing nature would win thence
    Some wooly innocence!
                —C. S. Lewis, *Poems,* 122

DAY 4

O God, our Father, we remember at this Christmas time how the eternal Word became flesh and dwelt among us.

We thank you that Jesus took our human body upon him, so that we can never again dare to despise or neglect or misuse the body, since you made it your dwelling-place.

We thank you that Jesus did a day's work like any working-man, that he knew the problem of living together in a family, that he knew the frustration and irritation of serving the public, that he had to earn a living, and to face all the wearing routine of everyday work and life and living, and so clothed each common task with glory.

We thank you that he shared in all happy social occasions, that he was at home at weddings and at dinners and at festivals in the homes of simple ordinary people like ourselves. Grant that we may ever remember that in his unseen risen presence he is a guest in every home.

We thank you that he knew what friendship means, that he had his own circle of those whom he wanted to be with him, that he knew too what it means to be let down, to suffer from disloyalty and from the failure of love.

We thank you that he too had to bear unfair criticism, prejudiced opposition, malicious and deliberate misunderstanding.

We thank you that whatever happens to us, he has been there before, and that, because he himself has gone through things, he is able to help those who are going through them.

Help us never to forget that he knows life, because he lived life, and that he is with us at all times to enable us to live victoriously.

This we ask for your love's sake. Amen.
—William Barclay, *A Barclay Prayer Book*, 16–17

DAY 5
The Baby in the Closet

My daughter, Amy, came bursting into my office one Sunday morning after church. She was six years old at the time, and trembling with some important piece of news. I quickly hung up my clergy robe and turned my attention to my daughter. "What is it, Amy?" I asked, hoping she hadn't found one of her brothers perched on the church steeple.

The words came tumbling out of her mouth. "Oh, Mom," she gasped. "Mom! We found baby Jesus in a closet and *guess what?*" She paused, trying to catch her breath. I held mine, too, uncertain what was coming next.

Amy let out a sigh. Her blue eyes grew wide and round. "We unwrapped the blanket he was in, and there, there on baby Jesus, we found a *belly button!*"

I began to breathe again. I wiped my hand across my mouth, so Amy couldn't see my smile. This was a very serious discovery, as far as she was concerned.

"Just like me, Mom, just like me. I never knew baby Jesus had a belly button just like me." She hiked up her T-shirt to make her point.

The baby Jesus doll doesn't get much use at our church. Every year, we have a live nativity scene during the Christmas pageant. A family from the church plays the part of the holy family. The doll serves as a stand-in, just in case the real baby gets sick at the last minute, or needs a diaper change. So far, we've never had to put the doll into action, so he sits in the closet, awaiting his debut.

And every Christmas, I am again filled with awe at the wonder of it all. I see the baby wrapped in a receiving blanket, the closest thing we have to swaddling cloths. I glance at the homemade holy family, dressed in strange concoctions of fabric, their faces glowing with joy. I watch the children of the church scramble for a better view, with their half-cocked tinsel halos and shepherd's headbands made of old pantyhose. I feel the brush of wings across my face and hear the faint sounds of an angel chorus mingled with the voices of my congregation, and together we sing, "Glory to God in the highest!" and I am there in the stable at Bethlehem.

But then Christmas is over, and it's back to life as usual. And days and days go by, and in the shuffle of my routine, I forget to take the time to wonder. I forget to marvel at this gift, until a child reminds me how.

I sat down next to Amy, pulled her onto my lap, and put my arms around her. "Yes, Amy," I said, pressing my cheek against her soft hair. "Baby Jesus was a baby just like you."

DAY 6
Incarnation

"The Word became flesh," wrote John, "and lived among us, . . . full of grace and truth" (John 1:14). That is what incarnation means. It is untheological. It is unsophisticated. It is undignified. But according to Christianity, it is the way things are.

All religions and philosophies that deny the reality or the significance of the material, the fleshly, the earthbound, are themselves denied. Moses at the burning bush was told to take off his shoes because the ground on which he stood was holy ground (Exodus 3:5), and incarnation means that all ground is holy ground because God not only made it but walked on it, ate and slept and worked and died on it. If we are saved anywhere, we are saved here. And what is saved is not some diaphanous distillation of our bodies and our earth, but our bodies and our earth themselves. Jerusalem becomes the New Jerusalem coming down out of heaven like a bride adorned for her husband (Revelation 21:2). Our bodies are sown perishable and raised imperishable (1 Corinthians 15:42).

One of the blunders religious people are particularly fond of making is the attempt to be more spiritual than God."

—Frederick Buechner, *Beyond Words*, 169

DAY 7

Breath Prayer: Close your eyes; take several slow, deep breaths; then silently pray this breath prayer in rhythm with your breathing. Repeat several times.

*Jesus, thank you
for becoming like me.*

— Light your Sabbath Celebration candle. Sit quietly for five minutes.
— Read the Bible passage for this week: Hebrews 2:17.
— Quietly reflect on the amazing way that God came to live among us in Jesus Christ, out of love.
— What has this Advent season meant to you? How have you celebrated the season? What do you imagine it will be like when Jesus returns to this world?
— In your journal, write about a special Christmas memory.
— Pray for a sense of wonder and joy during this time of year, and to carry that with you into the coming year.

One good hour may be worth a lifetime; an instant of returning to God may restore what has been lost in years of escaping from Him. (Abraham Joshua Heschel, 98)

ACKNOWLEDGMENTS

Excerpts from *The Book of a Thousand Prayers*, edited by Angela Ashwin. Copyright ©1996. Used by permission of The Zondervan Corporation.

Excerpts from *A Barclay Prayer Book*, by William Barclay. Copyright © 1990, 2003. Used by permission of SCM Press, London; and Westminster John Knox Press, Louisville, KY, USA.

Excerpts from "Manifesto: The Mad Farmer's Liberation Front" from *Collected Poems, 1957–1982*, by Wendell Berry. Copyright © 1973. Used by permission of the author.

"Summer Snow" by Kathleen Long Bostrom was previously published in *Voice of Many Waters: A Sacred Anthology for Today*, edited by Kay Snodgrass. Copyright © 1997, 2000 Kay Snodgrass. Used by permission of Geneva Press.

Excerpts from *Awed to Heaven, Rooted in Earth: Prayers of Walter Brueggemann*. Copyright © 2003 Augsburg Fortress. Reprinted by permission of Augsburg Fortress.

Excerpts from *Credo*, by William Sloane Coffin. Copyright © 2004 William Sloane Coffin. Used by permission of Westminster John Knox Press.

"i thank You God for most this amazing". Copyright 1950, © 1978, 1991 by the Trustees for the E. E. Cummings

Trust. Copyright © 1979 by George James Firmage, from *Complete Poems: 1904–1962* by E. E. Cummings, edited by George J. Firmage. Used by permission of Liveright Publishing Corporation.

Poems by MaryAnn McKibben Dana are reprinted by kind permission of the author.

Excerpt from "Affirmations" in *Earth Elegy: New and Selected Poems* by Margaret Gibson. Copyright © 1997 by Margaret Gibson. Used by permission of Louisiana State University Press.

Excerpts from *The Sabbath*, by Abraham Joshua Heschel. Copyright © 1951 by Abraham Joshua Heschel. Copyright renewed 1979 by Sylvia Heschel. Reprinted by permission of Farrar, Straus and Giroux, LLC.

"On a Theme from Nicolas of Cusa," "Relapse," and "Among the Oxen" from *Poems* by C. S. Lewis. Copyright © 1964 by the Executors of the Estate of C. S. Lewis and renewed 1992 by C. S. Lewis Pte. Ltd. Reprinted by permission of Harcourt Inc. and C. S. Lewis Pte. Ltd.

Excerpts from *Bread of Tomorrow: Prayers for the Church Year*, edited by Janet Morley. Copyright © 1992 SPCK. Used by permission of SPCK.

"Hope" from *Alive Together: New and Selected Poems* by Lisel Mueller. Copyright © 1996 by Lisel Mueller. Used by permission of Louisiana State University Press.

Excerpt from *Why I Wake Early: New Poems* by Mary Oliver. Copyright © 2004 by Mary Oliver. Reprinted by permission of Beacon Press, Boston.

"Ich glaube an Alles . . . / I believe in all that has never yet been spoken . . . ," "Gott spricht zu jedem . . . / God speaks to each of us . . . ," "Du bist die Zukunft . . . / You are the future . . . ," and "Denn sieh: sie werden leben und sich mehren . . . / There's also this to see . . ." are from *Rilke's Book of Hours: Love Poems to God* by Rainer Maria Rilke, translated by Anita Barrows and

Joanna Macy. Copyright © 1996 by Anita Barrows and Joanna Macy. Used by permission of Riverhead Books, an imprint of Penguin Group (USA) Inc., and Janklow & Nesbit Associates.

"December Solstice—Dawn" by J. Barrie Shepherd. Copyright © 2003 Christian Century. Reprinted with permission from the December 27, 2003, issue of *The Christian Century.*

"Recollection" by J. Barrie Shepherd. Copyright © 2004 *Theology Today.* Originally published in *Theology Today* 61 (2004): 360. Reprinted with publisher's permission.

Other poems by J. Barrie Shepherd are reprinted by kind permission of the author.

"Forgive Us," originally titled "Prayer of Confession," by Ann Weems is used by permission of Congregational Ministries Publishing, Mission Education and Promotion, Presbyterian Church (U.S.A.), 100 Witherspoon Street, Louisville, KY 40202.

Poems from *Kneeling in Bethlehem* by Ann Weems. Copyright © 1993 Ann Barr Weems. Used by permission of Westminster John Knox Press.

Poems from *Searching for Shalom: Resources for Creative Worship* by Ann Weems. Copyright © 1991 Ann Barr Weems. Used by permission of Westminster John Knox Press.

Excerpts from *The Complete Book of Christian Prayer.* Copyright © 1995 SPCK. Reprinted by permission of The Continuum International Publishing Group.

Excerpts from *A New Zealand Prayer Book: He Karakia Mihinare o Aotearoa.* Copyright © 1989 The General Secretary, The Anglican Church in Aotearoa, New Zealand and Polynesia. Used by permission of the Anglican Church in Aotearoa.

Excerpts from *The One Year Book of Personal Prayer: Inspirational Prayers and Thoughts for Each Day of the Year.* Copyright © 1991. Used by permission of Tyndale House Publishers, Inc.

WORKS CITED

Ashwin, Angela, ed. *The Book of a Thousand Prayers*. Grand Rapids, MI: Zondervan, 2002.

Barclay, William. *A Barclay Prayer Book*. Louisville, KY: Westminster John Knox Press, 2003.

Bernanos, Georges. *The Diary of a Country Priest: A Novel*. New York: Carroll & Graf, 2002.

Berry, Wendell. *Collected Poems, 1957–1982*. San Francisco: North Point Press, 1985.

Betz, Adrienne, ed. *Scholastic Treasury of Quotations for Children*. New York: Scholastic, 1998.

Brueggeman, Walter. *Awed to Heaven, Rooted in Earth: Prayers of Walter Brueggeman*. Edited by Edwin Searcy. Minneapolis, MN: Augsburg Fortress, 2003.

Buechner, Frederick. *Beyond Words: Daily Readings in the ABC's of Faith*. New York: HarperCollins, 2004.

Buechner, Frederick. *The Longing for Home: Reflections at Midlife*. New York: HarperCollins, 1996.

Buechner, Frederick. *Wishful Thinking: A Seeker's ABC*. San Francisco: HarperSanFrancisco, 1993.

Chittister, Joan. *Listen with the Heart: Sacred Moments in Everyday Life*. Lanham, MD: Sheed & Ward, 2003.

Coffin, William Sloane. *Credo*. Louisville, KY: Westminster John Knox Press, 2003.

The Complete Book of Christian Prayer. New York: Continuum, 1996.

Cummings, E. E. *Complete Poems 1904–1962.* Revised edition. Edited by George J. Firmage, New York: Liveright, 1994.

Dawn, Marva J. *Keeping the Sabbath Wholly: Ceasing, Resting, Embracing, Feasting.* Grand Rapids, MI: Wm. B. Eerdmans Publishing Co., 1989.

Dickinson, Emily. *The Complete Poems of Emily Dickinson.* New York: Back Bay Books, 1976.

Eerdmans Book of Christian Poetry. Grand Rapids: MI: Wm. B. Eerdmans Publishing Co., 1981.

Eliot, George. *Middlemarch.* Revised edition. New York: Penguin Books, 2003.

Gibson, Margaret. *Earth Elegy: New and Selected Poems.* Baton Rouge, LA: Louisiana State University Press, 1997.

Herbert, George. *The Complete English Works.* New York: Everyman's Library, 1995.

Heschel, Abraham Joshua. *The Sabbath.* New York: Farrar, Straus & Giroux, 1951.

The Hymnal 1982 according to the Use of the Episcopal Church. New York: The Church Hymnal Corp., 1985.

Kushner, Harold. *Living a Life That Matters.* New York: Anchor Books, 2002.

L'Engle, Madeleine. *Walking on Water: Reflections on Faith and Art.* New York: Bantam Books, 1980.

Lee, Harper. *To Kill a Mockingbird.* New York: Warner Books, 1982.

Lewis, C. S. *Poems.* Edited by Walter Hooper. New York: Harvest, 2002.

Llewellyn, Richard. *How Green Was My Valley.* New York: Scribner, 1997.

Longacre, Doris Janzen. *Living More with Less.* Scottdale, PA: Herald Press, 1980.

Looking for God in All the Right Places: Prayers and Poems to Comfort, Inspire, and Connect Humanity. Edited by June Cotner. Chicago: Loyola Press, 2004.

Morley, Janet, ed. *Bread of Tomorrow: Prayers for the Church Year.* Maryknoll, NY: Orbis Books, 1992.

Mueller, Lisel. *Alive Together: New and Selected Poems.* Baton Rouge, LA: Louisiana State University Press, 1996.

Muller, Wayne. *Sabbath: Finding Rest, Renewal, and Delight in Our Busy Lives.* New York: Bantam Books, 2000.

A New Zealand Prayer Book: He Karakia Mihinare O Aotearoa. San Francisco: HarperSanFrancisco, 1997.

Norris, Kathleen. *The Cloister Walk.* New York: Riverhead Books, 1996.

Oliver, Mary. *Why I Wake Early: New Poems.* Boston: Beacon Press, 2004.

Oman, Maggie, ed. *Prayers for Healing: 365 Blessings, Poems, and Meditations from around the World.* Berkeley, CA: Conari Press, 2000.

The One Year Book of Personal Prayer: Inspirational Prayers and Thoughts for Each Day of the Year. Carol Stream, IL: Tyndale, 1991.

Rilke, Rainer Maria. *Letters to a Young Poet.* Translated by M. D. Herter Norton. Revised edition. New York: W. W. Norton & Co., 1954.

Rilke, Rainer Maria. *Rilke's Book of Hours: Love Poems to God.* Edited by Anita Barrows and Joanna Macy. New York: Riverhead Books, 1997.

Shepherd, J. Barrie. "December Solstice—Dawn." *The Christian Century.* December 27, 2003.

Shepherd, J. Barrie. "Recollection." *Theology Today* 61 (2004): 360.

Snodgrass, Kay, ed. *Voice of Many Waters: A Sacred Anthology for Today.* Louisville, KY: Geneva Press, 2000.

Steinbeck, John. *East of Eden.* (New York: Penguin Books, 2002.

Thompson, Marjorie J. *Soul Feast: An Invitation to the Christian Spiritual Life*. Louisville, KY: Westminster John Knox Press, 1995.

Weems, Ann. *Kneeling in Bethlehem*. Philadelphia: Westminster Press, 1980.

Weems, Ann. *Searching for Shalom: Resources for Creative Worship*. Louisville, KY: Westminster John Knox Press, 1991.

The Westminster Collection of Christian Quotations. Compiled by Martin Manser. Louisville, KY: Westminster John Knox Press, 2001.

Winter, Miriam Therese. *WomanPrayer, WomanSong: Resources for Ritual*. Oak Park, IL: Meyer Stone Books, 1987.